Comments on other *Amazing Stories* from readers & reviewers

"*Tightly written volumes filled with lots of wit and humour about famous and infamous Canadians.*"
Eric Shackleton, *The Globe and Mail*

"*The heightened sense of drama and intrigue, combined with a good dose of human interest is what sets* Amazing Stories *apart.*"
Pamela Klaffke, *Calgary Herald*

"*This is popular history as it should be... For this price, buy two and give one to a friend.*"
Terry Cook, a reader from Ottawa, on **Rebel Women**

"*Glasner creates the moment of the explosion itself in graphic detail...she builds detail upon gruesome detail to create a convincingly authentic picture.*"
Peggy McKinnon, *The Sunday Herald*, on **The Halifax Explosion**

"*It was wonderful...I found I could not put it down. I was sorry when it was completed.*"
Dorothy F. from Manitoba on **Marie-Anne Lagimodière**

"*Stories are rich in description, and bristle with a clever, stylish realness.*"
Mark Weber, *Central Alberta Advisor*, on **Ghost Town Stories II**

"*A compelling read. Bertin...has selected only the most intriguing tales, which she narrates with a wealth of detail.*"
Joyce Glasner, *New Brunswick Reader*, on **Strange Events**

"*The resulting book is one readers will want to share with all the women in their lives.*"
Lynn Martel, *Rocky Mountain Outlook*, on **Women Explorers**

AMAZING STORIES

TORONTO MURDERS

AMAZING STORIES

TORONTO MURDERS
Mysteries, Crimes, and Scandals

CRIME/MYSTERY
by Susan McNicoll

PUBLISHED BY ALTITUDE PUBLISHING CANADA LTD.
1500 Railway Avenue, Canmore, Alberta T1W 1P6
www.altitudepublishing.com
www.amazingstories.ca
1-800-957-6888

Copyright 2005 © Susan McNicoll
All rights reserved
First published 2005

Extreme care has been taken to ensure that all information presented in this book is accurate and up to date. Neither the author nor the publisher can be held responsible for any errors.

Publisher	Stephen Hutchings
Associate Publisher	Kara Turner
Series Editor	Jill Foran
Editor	Georgina Montgomery
Digital Photo Colouring	Bryan Pezzi

We acknowledge the financial support of the Government of Canada through the Book Publishing Industry Development Program (BPIDP) for our publishing activities.

Altitude GreenTree Program
Altitude Publishing will plant twice as many trees as were used in the manufacturing of this product.

National Library of Canada Cataloguing in Publication Data

McNicoll, Susan
   Toronto murders / Susan McNicoll.

(Amazing stories)
ISBN 1-55439-031-1

   1. Murder--Ontario--Toronto Region--History. I. Title. II. Series: Amazing stories (Calgary, Alta.)

HV6535.C33T67 2005   364.152'3'09713542   C2005-903211-1

Amazing Stories® is a registered trademark of Altitude Publishing Canada Ltd.

Printed and bound in Canada by Friesens
2 4 6 8 9 7 5 3 1

For Hans
who many years ago reached
deep inside me and found my soul.

Contents

Prologue 11
Chapter 1 Robbing the Hangman 13
Chapter 2 He Said, She Said 31
Chapter 3 Mum's the Word 51
Chapter 4 Murder and Bigotry 71
Chapter 5 My Brother's Keeper. 89
Chapter 6 Death by Alcohol 108
Futher Reading 126

Prologue

Robert sat quietly on the steps of the wagon shop, "a gun across his knees and a shot pouch over his shoulder." The sun shone brightly, making the late September day feel warm in the dusty village of Lambton Mills. It was 11:30 a.m. as Alfred Rook walked along Dundas Street and stopped to talk to the young man.

"My name being Rook, I thought to crack a joke with him," Alfred later stated. "I said to him, 'Robert, you must not shoot any of those rooks [crows] around here.'"

"I am looking for other game" was the reply.

Fifteen minutes later, when his younger brother, Edward, approached the wagon shop from his home up the street, Robert rose from the steps and walked purposefully towards him.

"I have been waiting for you a good while, you bugger, and now I have got you," Robert called out. He raised his gun and, as Edward threw his hands up and cried, "Oh, don't!" Robert pulled the trigger. Then, for good measure, he moved closer to the dying man and shot him again.

Robert turned and began to walk calmly down the street, ignoring the commotion behind him as someone rushed to his brother's aid. When he was at least 45 metres away, next to the church, he stopped and took a small vial from his pocket.

Toronto Murders

He pulled out the cork, tilted his head back and poured the contents down his throat. Then, throwing aside the tiny bottle, he strode on.

Chapter 1
Robbing the Hangman

Public hanging was still a spectator sport in Canada in 1864, staged outside prison walls. On February 23 of that year, the spectators in the fields surrounding Toronto Gaol were growing restless. The scaffold, which had loomed large and foreboding the day before, had disappeared and rumours were rolling through the crowd. One was that the sentenced man, William Greenwood, had escaped and left a dead body in his cell to take his place. Another was that his friends had succeeded in a daring rescue of him. And still a third was that a last-minute reprieve had been granted.

What was the truth?

The end of this story, it turns out, was as full of drama as all the parts leading up to it.

Toronto Murders

* * *

Although at the time of his trial he looked considerably older than his years, William Greenwood was only 26. He was born on January 6, 1838, in the village of Long Preston in England's Yorkshire County. His father was a gardener from whom William acquired a passion for flowers.

"I left school of my own accord when about ten years of age, and have been supporting myself ever since," William was later to write.

After three or four years of various jobs, he decided to follow his father's trade as a gardener. He found work in Liverpool, but then "concluded," as he put it, "to try my fortune in America." He was 17 when he arrived in Toronto in 1855, working for the next two years at Leslie's Nurseries on Kingston Road.

After a year at various jobs, William began working for a market gardener, John Sedgwick, who not only gave him a job but, in November 1858, his only daughter in marriage. Charlotte was 16 years old. For a year and a half, William and Charlotte lived and worked with her father, until William grew restless. He looked around for another job and soon found a good position as a gardener for the Honourable John Hilyard Cameron, a federal Member of Parliament. William moved his family into a cottage on the property. They were together there for 16 months until Charlotte decided to leave, taking their two

Robbing the Hangman

children with her to live at her mother's. According to William, she moved out so they could save money for him to start a business, but in fact he seldom saw them from that point on. William moved from the cottage into the main house.

Almost from the time he started working at the Camerons', William's sexual conquests began. According to him, though, they were never his idea. One of his paramours was Agnes Marshall, a servant at the house. In William's words, she seduced him.

"Late in September 1862, on a Sunday, I was shaving in the upper kitchen. Mr. and Mrs. Cameron had gone out to church. They were waited on to the door by Agnes Marshall. She came immediately down stairs and took up my brush and lathered the side of my face; I was sitting with my razor in my hand. I told her if she did not quit I would give her a good shaking; she said I was not able; I told her I would show her; I immediately pulled her, and she, I may say with no reluctance, entered my bedroom. On that occasion for the first time in my life, I had connection [intercourse] with her.

"This familiarity was too often indulged in. Every time she met me she would strike me in the stomach and tempt me in every way. She tried to induce me to leave my wife and go with her to the States. This I refused to do."

However, five months after their first "criminal connection" (as the newspapers put it), Agnes became very ill. It was February 20, 1863, and the rumour going around the house was that she had had a child, although no one had actually seen the baby. A doctor was brought in to treat her, but she would not let him examine her and just told him it was "women's problems." She was bedridden, but became sicker with each passing day. Eventually she was taken to hospital, where she died on March 20.

* * *

It was less than a month later — on April 15, 1863 — that Francis Duckett was wakened in the middle of the night by his wife, Elizabeth. She had heard unusual noises coming from the house immediately adjacent to theirs. Mr. Duckett became suspicious, too, and grew concerned that someone was "taking out the furniture." The intruder must have heard the Ducketts at the same time, for he quickly left the house, slamming the front door and heading up the street. Duckett followed the man, but although he could identify the coat he was wearing, he did not get a clear look at his face before the man spotted him and ran away.

Still concerned, Duckett went in search of a policeman. When he and Constable John King returned to the house at 156 Sayer (later Chestnut) Street, they found the door unlocked and, once inside, a strong smell of something burning. The house was dark and filling with smoke. King went into the bedroom, pulled up the valance of the bed, and found a candlestick leaning against the edge of the mattress. The fire was already spreading quickly. Duckett got a pail of water for

Robbing the Hangman

King and then ran outside to give the alarm. With the smoke becoming denser, King tried to remove the bed coverings. It was then he found a woman lying dead in the bed.

"She was quite cold," he later testified. "I carried the body into the front room ... and [then] succeeded in extinguishing the fire."

It was not his only discovery. Searching the house, he came upon the body of a newborn baby boy wrapped up in towelling and a flour bag and tucked in a kitchen cupboard. The umbilical cord had not been tied off, which led authorities to believe there was no medical attendance at his birth. The baby had bled to death. It became obvious that the fire was no accident and, as *The Globe and Mail* reported, "that the bed had been set fire to, in order that the evidence of some dark deed might be concealed."

An inquest was begun the next day, taking place in the local tavern. It was quickly established that the woman, Catherine Walsh, had been strangled to death not long after giving birth to a son. She was said to be married to a Matthew McNulty, but later evidence showed that was not so and that he had moved to the United States some time before. Clearly, then, he could not have been the father of the child.

From Ireland originally, Catherine had moved to Canada 10 years earlier. Approximately 32 years old at the time of her death, she was described as an attractive woman with auburn hair. Also once a servant at the Cameron house, she was remembered for being clean and tidy. At the time of her death, Catherine had been wearing a brown raglan jacket over a nightgown and chemise. King noted that both the latter were saturated with blood from the waist down. Her face was swollen and discoloured and her tongue protruding.

Catherine had left the Camerons' employ in 1862 and moved into the small house on Sayer Street. The house had apparently been rented in the autumn of 1862 by a man who called himself William Green. When a search of the house turned up a novel called *The English Country Gentleman*, in which was pencilled the name "Wm. Greenwood," police decided to question William. On April 17, 1863 — two days after the fire — they found a coat with blood stains on it in his room in the Cameron house.

William appeared at Catherine's inquest somewhat reluctantly. *The Globe and Mail* described the young man as being 5 feet 9 inches tall and stocky, with "an open countenance, ruddy cheeks, grey or dark blue eyes and dark curly hair with dark whiskers and moustache." In a statement he would later regret, William claimed never to have been inside Catherine's house. He also insisted that one of his hobbies was fighting game cocks and that the blood on his coat was a result of carrying a bird in his arms after a fight.

On Saturday, April 18, Catherine Walsh and her baby son were placed into one coffin and buried. The only mourner was Edward Duckett. On the same day, the inquest heard some damning testimony from George States, a coachman for the Cayley family. States often drove Mrs. Cayley to visit

Robbing the Hangman

at the Cameron house. During those visits, he ate with the servants and, over almost four years, had come to know Catherine quite well. After she left her job at the Camerons', States told the inquest, Catherine supported herself by sewing and was sometimes hired in this capacity by Mrs. Cayley. On such occasions, she would stay at the house for a day or two until her work was finished. One of these times was at the beginning of April 1863. When Catherine departed in the evening to return to Sayer Street, States offered to go part of the way with her "as the road was dark and lonely" — though it seems he had another motive too. While walking from the Cayley house above the cemetery towards Parliament Street, he asked her if she would mind "keeping company" (marrying) with him.

"I thought she would make me a comfortable wife. When I asked her the question, she replied 'No' but added 'I have something very serious to tell you.'" Catherine then told him she was "in the family way."

"I told her I was very sorry for her troubles," States continued, "and asked her who was the man — the father of the child. She then said she was very sorry as it was a married man ... Mr. Cameron's gardener." Catherine also told States that if she "did not get over it all right," he could tell someone her secret.

When States heard who had been found murdered, he did just that.

The jury at the inquest concluded that Catherine Walsh

Toronto Murders

had been strangled to death by William Greenwood on the night of April 14 or the morning of April 15. A trial date was set for October. The newspapers reported that the accused looked like the most unconcerned person in the room.

It looked like the case was over but it was actually only just beginning.

* * *

The subject of Agnes Marshall and her illness and death had been front and centre during the inquest for Catherine Walsh — and for her baby (who, the inquest had found, "died from the want of proper care and attention at its birth"). If Agnes had also had a child, what happened to it? Infanticide was not uncommon in Canada in the 1800s and the mothers were looked on very leniently, with the courts usually turning a blind eye. Most of the women who found themselves pregnant were young, single, and poor. Many babies of servants ended up discarded in "privies" (outhouses) or rubbish heaps.

"The guilty secret of more than a few respectable households was the paternity of a child born to a servant," Carolyn Strange writes in her book, *Toronto's Girl Problem: The Perils and Pleasures of the City, 1880–1930*. "If she disposed of the child, everyone involved might escape shame."

However, the same leniency was not given to the father if he took the same action. Because Agnes Marshall and her pregnancy were now in the spotlight, the authorities felt that if a baby had existed, it had to be found. With that mission, three policemen conducted a thorough search of the Cameron house and property on April 21. Their efforts were not in vain. Partially buried in the soil of the privy at the back of the house, the policemen found the body of a baby boy, wrapped in a piece of cloth. A piece of twine was tied around the baby's neck, with a brick attached to the other end in the hopes of sinking the body into the soil.

Another inquest was launched into this baby's death and, at the same time, the body of Agnes Marshall was ordered exhumed so her cause of death could be determined. Both inquests took place during the last few days of April and the first few days of May 1863.

The inquest heard that this was not Agnes's first child. Margaret McCaul, a former cook at the Cameron house, swore that Agnes had given birth to a child in a room off the butler's pantry a year earlier — a baby that wasn't seen after that. William Greenwood had been present at that birth.

Dr. James Bovell told the inquest that Agnes's death "was caused by having a birth and great loss of blood." The death of her baby was more ominous. The jury concluded that it had been born alive but went to its death by violence. At whose hands this crime had been committed they didn't have sufficient evidence to show, though they pointed to the prisoner, William Greenwood, as being an accessory to the concealment of its birth.

Toronto Murders

* * *

William's trial for the murder of Catherine Walsh began on October 31, 1863, before Justice Adam Wilson. Early testimony was taken up with doctors showing that Catherine had given birth and that there was no doubt she was strangled to death. One of the strongest witnesses for the prosecution was Catherine's former neighbour, Elizabeth Duckett. She was referred to in the papers as the "coloured witness," but, far more importantly, she proved to be a strong woman who was very sure of what she had seen.

And what she had seen was that William Greenwood — contrary to his denials — frequently visited next door. Elizabeth told the jury, for example, that William and Catherine came over one evening to ask if Francis, her husband, would whitewash their house for them. He did and they paid for the job. She also saw William moving furniture into the house and believed the two were married. As well, she said William often arrived at the house after 10:00 at night and left early in the morning. On the night of the murder, she said she saw the man out on the street walking away from the house. While she could not positively identify William in the darkness, she swore the man had on a coat exactly like the one the prosecution showed her as belonging to William. And in identifying the accused as the man who had been with Catherine, Elizabeth said she recognized him partly because of a peculiar tooth he had.

Robbing the Hangman

The blood on the coat drew attention from both the prosecution and the defence. In addition to his game-fighting cock story, William had told another person that the blood came from a cow that had calved a short time before at the Camerons'. At the same time, the defence even pointed to the fact that their client had punched Catherine with enough force one night to knock out a tooth. That, they said, was perhaps how the blood got on his clothes.

Although DNA testing did not exist back in 1863, there was more technology than William had counted on. Dr. Bovell, with the help of a powerful microscope, examined the blood on the coat. As he subsequently testified, "The particles of the blood discovered could not be the blood of any bird. I have experimented with the blood of a cow, that of a horse and that of a human being, and am of the opinion that the particles found on the coat were those of human blood."

From a bloody tooth? No, said a second physician.

"I have no doubt," Dr. James Phillibrick told the court, "that it came from some portion of the mucous surface of a human being; it is such as would come from a woman in delivery."

The prosecution brought forward more damning evidence. As well as the novel inscribed with William's name found in Catherine's house, the candlestick used in the attempt to burn the place down was identified as being exactly like the ones in the servants' rooms at the Cameron house. A special stick was also found there and identified by the Camerons' coachman as belonging to William (made by him, apparently, for "thrashing cats"). The coachman also said that William had knocked out one of Catherine's teeth while she was living at the Cameron house because she reprimanded him for coming in after the curfew time of 10 p.m., forcing her to have to wait up for him to let him in. The servants at the Camerons' had to be home by that hour every night, but testimony was also given by others to show that William often went out after 10:00, leaving and coming back in through his bedroom window.

It was not going well for William at the trial until the question of time of death arose. The doctors put it at somewhere between 7 and 9 p.m. One witness swore that William had been at her house during that time. Mary Ann Rapley was a recent widow who lived in a house opposite the Camerons', and she appeared to know William well. It was reported that she visited him in jail after the murder, walking up to him, kissing him, and generally being very affectionate. She also admitted to contributing $5 to a defence fund for William. However, on cross-examination, Rapley acknowledged that William was gone from her house for long periods during the time in question, especially between 7 and 8 p.m. That left a large window of opportunity for William to kill Catherine — though it also muddied the waters enough to leave doubt in the mind of the jurors.

The defence took full advantage of this, and also tried

Robbing the Hangman

to discredit Elizabeth Duckett's testimony by having William open his mouth and show his teeth to the jury. There was no "peculiar" tooth. In only an hour of deliberation, the jury returned with a "not guilty" verdict.

The public outcry was tremendous. An editorial in *The Globe and Mail* intoned, "Had our law permitted it, the verdict would not have been 'not guilty' but 'not proven' ... Had the jury been required by law to say that the prisoner was innocent, they would scarcely have done so. He has very narrowly escaped."

William Greenwood wasn't yet totally in the clear, however. He was still charged with setting the fire, and arson was still a capital offence in those days, although the death sentence was seldom imposed.

The arson trial began on William's birthday, January 6, 1864. Justice J. Wilson presided, with Thomas Galt heading the prosecution. Defending William were M.C. Cameron (no relation to William's previous employer) and John Canavan. Having won an acquittal for murder, the defence probably expected the same result with the arson case, especially since most of the evidence remained the same. But there was one glaring difference. Prosecutor Galt informed the jury that William had had a tooth extracted from his mouth by the jail physician a few days before the murder trial. Galt then brought several witnesses forward who remembered William having a strange tooth when he was first arrested. This piece of evidence more than any other was likely responsible for the jury finding William guilty of arson. He was sentenced to seven years in prison.

Authorities quickly moved to again charge William Greenwood with murder, this time of Agnes Marshall's baby. The third trial began on January 22, 1864. Servants told the court that Agnes had been a great favourite with the Cameron family. Indeed, Mrs. Cameron testified to that and also talked about how ill Agnes had been before they finally forced her to go into hospital. On the day she became ill, she had apparently been in the water closet (indoor bathroom) for three hours, with no one but William attending to her. According to the Camerons' butler, Hugh Lamont, at one point not long before Agnes came out, he saw William returning to the kitchen from the yard with an empty bucket. Lamont also stated that he had seen William strike Agnes many times in the past and that she seemed afraid of him. When he had spoken up to William about it, William told him to mind his own business.

Testimony also showed that the baby found buried on the Cameron property had been born alive before being killed, either by smothering or drowning. He had weighed almost 7 pounds and was 21 inches long, with a full head of black hair.

After only two days, during which no witnesses were called for the defence, the jury took three hours before rendering a "guilty" verdict. For the briefest moment, William lost his cool as the blood drained from his face and he clutched

Robbing the Hangman

the rail of the dock. The judge asked him if he had anything to say before sentence would be pronounced.

"I am not guilty, my lord," William replied. "I am perfectly innocent and I could make a statement to you which would convince you but I will not say anything now."

A few days after the second murder trial, Francis Duckett received a letter signed "A Friend of Greenwood." It stated, among other things, that unless he and his wife left town by January 30, they would both be murdered. "Duckett has taken legal advice in the matter, and is prepared to deal with any who may wish to make away with him," *The Globe and Mail* reported.

Following his conviction, William's lawyers immediately announced they would petition for a new trial. The facts of the case were reviewed extensively and some witnesses appeared on February 11, 1864. One of these was Constable John King, who was present when the body of Agnes's baby was found. He testified that he had kept part of the twine that was tied around the baby's neck and searched the Cameron home for corresponding twine. Though the search of the rest of the house came up empty, the search of William's room did not. In a locked box in the room, he found a piece of twine exactly like the one on the small body.

William later admitted removing the body of Agnes's child from the water closet, but maintained he did not kill it and did not know how it was killed. He wrote, "I am satisfied that she had children before, and was very loose in her

Toronto Murders

morals." He said a similar thing about Catherine Walsh in a letter to his lawyer, adding that the character of the two women "was not good, and there is other men could tell you that as well as me, if they like to do so."

The two Justices and one Chief Justice who reviewed the application for a new trial turned down the request. Pleas to the premier of Ontario and the governor general also failed, and the hanging was scheduled to take place at 10 a.m. on February 23, 1864.

* * *

A public hanging in the early 1800s was an event not to be missed. People would travel from miles away to witness one, often coming to town the night before to vie for the best location from which to watch the killer "suffer the extreme penalty of the law." They — men, women, and children — would bring their lunches with them and make a social outing out of it. This was much the same scene for William Greenwood's hanging.

"There were thousands of strangers in the city who had arrived the previous night," a *Globe and Mail* article reported, "and long before daybreak all quiet of the city was abolished by the rattle of farmer's waggons [sic] coming in from all parts of the surrounding country loaded with men, women and children to witness the execution ... They wended their way, with the first streak of dawn, to the Old Fair Green, in order to

Robbing the Hangman

select good positions from which to see the unfortunate man launched into eternity."

Their excitement was to turn to disappointment when they saw that the scaffold was no longer there. Rumours began to run through the crowd and some of them had a hint of truth in them. For instance, the governor of the jail had received a tip that William's friends were planning to make a rescue attempt. And, in a way, William had escaped.

According to Reverend Alex Sanson, he left William at 10 p.m. the night before the execution. The guard in charge of the wing then also left to take care of some preparations for the hanging. When he returned 15 minutes later, he found William hanging from the window of his cell, having used a long towel to end his life. William had obviously planned this for a while, because he had to have sneaked in the towel from elsewhere in the prison. The deed itself could not have been easy either, as the window of the cell was not even two metres above the floor.

"In order, therefore, to strangle himself he was compelled to lie down, so that the towel might have the desired effect upon his neck," *The Globe and Mail* reported. "He seems even to have clutched the bed in his hands and have pulled himself as it were with all his strength upon the towel, so that there might not be any chance of his failing to put his awful intention into execution."

The crowd around the jail heard of Greenwood's suicide, but they were not convinced. Many of them thought it was a hoax by prison officials to keep people away from the execution. Others believed he had escaped and the dead body found in his cell was not his, but was placed there with the idea "that it would be taken as his." The latter theory was so rampant and the crowd so restless, authorities decided the body would have to be displayed at the "dead house" (morgue). Thousands of people then rushed to see the body and many were injured in the ensuing pandemonium.

William would have enjoyed the notoriety. Two doctors, both coroners, fought over the right to do the autopsy and carried their fight to the inquest. While there was a lot of finger-pointing, Rev. Sanson was quoted as saying that he always doubted William's sincerity. "He had strong powers of deception," felt Sanson.

Nevertheless, William protested his innocence to the end. In a letter for his lawyer, John Canavan, he wrote, "I have said to the prisoners in the wing that I would never go to the scaffold an innocent man. I told them if I was found guilty of any murder that I was charged with I would not go over that wall alive."

That might have been the only time William Greenwood had told the truth.

Chapter 2
He Said, She Said

He said: "When the housekeeper was thrown down the cellar, after being knocked down, Grace Marks followed him into the cellar, and brought a piece of white cloth with her; he held the housekeeper's hands, she being then insensible, and Grace Marks tied the cloth tight round her neck and strangled her."

She said: "He presently came to me and said he had thrown her down the cellar and he said he wanted a handkerchief. I asked him what for, he said never mind, she is not dead yet. I gave him a piece of white cloth and followed him to the trap door ... he said you can't come down here, went down himself and shut the trap door after him."

Whether you believed James McDermott or Grace Marks, two people were dead and someone was not telling the truth.

Toronto Murders

* * *

In July 1843, the same month she turned 16, Grace Marks began working as a servant for Thomas Kinnear. A single man, Kinnear had retired early on from the army because of ill health and had lived in the area for many years. He was well thought of among his neighbours. His house was on the west side of Yonge Street in Richmond Hill, set 100 metres in from the road. Grace had been working as a servant elsewhere for three years when Kinnear's housekeeper, Nancy Montgomery, met her working for a shoemaker on Lot Street (shortly after renamed Queen Street). Nancy hired Grace, offering to pay her $3 a month, with room and board provided.

When Grace arrived at her new job, James McDermott had already been there a week. James was only 20 years old and, like Grace, had been born in Ireland. When he came to Canada, he first worked on board steamers running between Quebec and Montreal. Then in 1840 he enlisted as a private in the 1st Provincial Regiment of the Province of Lower Canada. When the regiment was disbanded two years later, James became a servant to a captain in the Glengarry Light Infantry Company, stationed in both Ontario and Quebec. Discharged a year later, he moved to Toronto. At the end of June, hearing Kinnear wanted a servant, James went to the house and was hired by Nancy.

He Said, She Said

James McDermott stood about 160 cm tall and was "of slender make, swarthy, and of a forbidding aspect," a reporter for the *British Colonist* later wrote. The same article noted that "Grace Marks, the female, although wholly devoid of education, possesses good features, and in point of personal appearance, is much superior to her paramour." Whether James and Grace were ever "paramours" would never be completely decided. However, they were left alone together a great deal because Montgomery spent most of her days, and many of her nights, catering to Kinnear.

"He [McDermott] told me he was positive that Kinnear and the housekeeper, Nancy, slept together," Grace would later state in one of her confessions. "I was determined to find it out, and I was afterwards convinced that they did so, for her bed was never slept in except when Mr. Kinnear was absent, and then I slept with her."

Nancy Montgomery had worked for Kinnear for a couple of years. She had been pregnant when he hired her and gave birth at a neighbour's house not long after. Following a five-month absence during which, she said, the baby had died, she returned to work for Kinnear.

Grace would also later say that James and Nancy did not get along, and that Nancy often said he wasn't doing his job properly. In fact, only two weeks after his arrival, James was given two weeks' notice and told to leave on the Sunday (July 30, 1843). He claimed to be happy about it.

"He often after this told me he was glad he was going,"

Toronto Murders

Grace said, "as he did not wish any longer to live with a parcel of whores, but would have satisfaction before he went."

However, James had his story too. According to him, Grace and the housekeeper often quarrelled. He also said that Grace told him the housekeeper had threatened to send her away, but that Grace said to him, "Now, McDermott, I am not going to leave in this way."

This may or may not have been true, but Grace certainly felt Nancy put on airs and thought herself better than the other servants.

* * *

Kinnear had decided to go into Toronto on Thursday, July 27, to collect a fairly large sum of money (reportedly his twice a year payment from the army). He then planned to return home on the Saturday. When James heard this, he (in Grace's version) hatched a murderous scheme. He would kill Nancy before Kinnear got home, and then shoot Kinnear. At that point, with all the money and valuables he could carry, James would escape to the United States. He asked Grace to help him. Whether she really agreed to or not is unclear.

As it happened, Kinnear deposited the money in his Toronto bank and had very little on him when he returned home. But once the wheels of the plan had been set into motion, there was no turning back.

On the Friday morning after breakfast, Nancy sent Grace

He Said, She Said

with a message for James that he was to leave that afternoon. When Grace told him, he said, "Tell Nancy I shall go on Saturday morning." Grace also quoted him as saying, "Damn her, is that what she is at! I'll kill her before morning."

James Walsh, 14, lived with his father in a cottage on Kinnear's farm and often ran errands for him. On the Friday he was there from mid-afternoon well into the evening, "playing his fife, at the request of the housekeeper." James McDermott had often bragged of his dancing, so Walsh and Nancy had encouraged him to do so. He said he was unwell and refused. At 10:30 p.m., when Nancy took a candle to go to bed, James motioned for the Walsh boy to leave, even walking him nearly all the way home. James returned to the house, with the aim of killing Nancy that night by hitting her head with the back of an axe while she slept. However, with Kinnear away and Nancy therefore sleeping with Grace, the young woman begged James to wait until morning because she was afraid he would accidentally hit her instead.

In James's version, it was really Grace who had wanted him to murder Nancy that night, but he couldn't bring himself to do it. The next morning, he said, Grace even called him a coward.

* * *

At about 7 a.m. on Saturday, James made his move when Grace was going to the pump for water. When she turned

Toronto Murders

around, Grace later testified, she saw that James had grabbed hold of Nancy and was dragging her through the yard. He was yelling at her, "Grace, you promised to help me! Come and open the trap door and I will throw her in the cellar." According to Grace, "being frightened," she refused to do so.

* * *

Jonathon Jefferson, the local butcher, arrived at the Kinnear house as he always did on the Saturday morning. He was met by Grace who told him they did not need any meat. He was puzzled because they always took some. He asked for Mr. Kinnear or the housekeeper, but was told neither of them was available, "but no matter, they wanted no meat."

Meanwhile, Thomas Kinnear was making his way back home by wagon from Toronto. When he arrived, he asked for Nancy but was told she had gone to a neighbour's house. Grace then asked if he would like something to eat. Kinnear asked if the butcher had been by with fresh meat, Grace said no. He settled for lunch of tea, toast, and eggs, after which he went to bed for a sleep.

"McDermott said 'I'll go in now and kill him, if you'll assist me,'" Grace later recounted in her version of events. "I said, 'Of course, McDermott, I will, as I have promised you.'" But then James decided to wait until dark.

Kinnear had something to eat at 7 p.m. and was reading a book in the living room when James went in to tell him he

He Said, She Said

had found some scratches on his new saddle. He persuaded Kinnear to go with him to the harness room to look at it. Grace was putting dishes away in the back kitchen when she heard a gun shot.

"I ran into the [front] kitchen and saw Mr. Kinnear lying dead on the floor, and McDermott standing over him," Grace said. "The double-barrelled gun was on the floor. When I saw this, I attempted to run out. He said, 'Damn you, come back and open the trap door!' I said, 'I won't.' He said, 'You shall, after having promised to assist me!' Knowing that I had promised, I then opened the trap door, and McDermott threw the body down. I was so frightened that I ran out of the front door into the lawn, went around into the back kitchen, and as I was standing at the door, McDermott came out of the front kitchen door into the yard and fired at me. The ball did not hit me but lodged in the jam of the door. I fainted."

James revived her, Grace said, telling her he had not meant to hurt her and that he thought the gun was empty. Shortly afterwards, the Walsh boy showed up at the house and was talking with Grace. She and James told him that Kinnear and Nancy were out. On hearing a chain rattle in the stable — the chain with which Kinnear's horse was usually tied — the boy asked about it. James told him it was the colt rattling the chain because it was upset at the horse being away. Walsh, however, knowing the colt was never tied with the chain, thought this strange. When he asked where Nancy had gone, Grace told him a neighbour had come and asked

Nancy to go and help with someone who was sick. When Walsh asked how they went, he was told they took Kinnear's horse and rode over together. The boy was struck by this apparent contradiction (how could they take Kinnear's horse if Kinnear himself was away on it?), but he finally left.

James Newton was not so easily put off. He had known Kinnear for seven years and they were frequent visitors at each other's house. When Newton arrived at Kinnear's house on Sunday morning he found everything quiet and no one around. He walked around the house and the garden. Seeing none of the servants, he went around to the front door and knocked. He went to the Walsh cottage, but they knew nothing. Newton returned to the main house and walked through it. He could find nothing of Kinnear, but did notice the place was in disarray — and that a few drops of blood were on the door between the hall and the kitchen. At 4 p.m., very concerned, he went to a neighbour, Francis Boyd, and persuaded him to return to Kinnear's with him. The two of them went through the house, including the cellar. There they discovered Kinnear, sprawled out on his back, dead from a chest wound. Blood had seeped through the shirt and tartan vest he was wearing.

Officials and a coroner were sent for and word of the murder spread quickly through the region. In no time, suspicion fell on the three missing servants.

That night in Toronto, Frederick Chase Capreol first heard about the murder from his children on their return

He Said, She Said

from an evening church service. Kinnear had been a close friend of Capreol's and as soon as he got the news he grabbed his hat and rushed from his house on Wellington Street to the police station. When he asked an officer and a detective what was going to be done to catch the killers, he was told "Nothing," until maybe the morning.

"But the morning will be too late to start about it," Capreol protested. "The rascals could be in the States by that time."

He was told that the police had no authority to do anything.

Frustrated, Capreol went back out onto the street and questioned a number of people who were milling about talking of the murder. He discovered that a man and woman had been seen in a wagon going at high speed along Vaughan Road. Capreol felt sure there was a connection, and he also felt sure he knew where they had been heading. On the spot, he decided to go after them and capture them himself. First he needed the authority to do so.

He dashed to the mayor's house. Although all the lights were off and Henry Sherwood and his family had obviously retired for the night, Capreol wasn't to be stopped. The servant who answered the door wouldn't let him in, saying the mayor was unavailable, but Capreol persisted in asking to see him. At that point, Sherwood himself appeared at the upstairs window.

"If you will give authority to pursue the murderers,"

Toronto Murders

Capreol called to the mayor, "I feel confident I can bring them back within two days. All I ask is your authority. I will bear all the expense myself."

Sherwood replied that something could be done in the morning and detectives sent after them. And with that, he shut the window.

The stumbling block through all of this seemed to be that because the murder took place in Richmond Hill, no one in Toronto was willing to authorize any action or spend any money in pursuing the suspects. Capreol realized he was on his own. Undeterred, he headed to the Church Street wharf and *The Transit*, a boat that made the trip to Lewiston, New York, regularly. Capreol found Captain Richardson, skipper of the vessel, and asked him to "get up steam immediately."

"Have you got one hundred dollars about you?" the captain asked. "Yes," Capreol answered. "I will give you a cheque right away for the amount if you must be paid in advance, although I think the charge exorbitant merely to go across the lake."

But the captain was having none of it. He demanded cash — even when Capreol explained why he needed to get to Lewiston immediately. Handing over all the cash he had, $13, Capreol told Richardson he'd be back in an hour and to have the boat up and running.

As luck would have it, Capreol ran into a wealthy friend on the street and appealed to him for the money. The luck stopped there. "I don't exactly care to advance money on

He Said, She Said

such a hare-brained scheme as yours," the friend said. "Leave it to the authorities."

Capreol hurried off to find someone else to help him. He thought of Alexander Ogilvie who lived above his store on the south side of King Street, a few doors west of Yonge Street. Rattling on the front doors of the store brought no reply and the amateur detective realized Ogilvie was upstairs at the rear of the building. Capreol went to the back, but met with solid gates and a high brick wall. Fuelled now by a frenzied determination, he made several attempts to scale the wall, but each time fell to the ground because he was unable to get a grasp anywhere along the wall's smooth surface. Finally, he took out his penknife and scraped away enough mortar between some of the bricks to make small finger and toe holds. Several more falls later, and now with his clothes ripped and his hands bleeding, Capreol made it over the wall and into Ogilvie's back yard. It was now 11:30 p.m. At the back of the building, he banged loudly for 10 minutes but got no reply. He was almost out of initiative — but not quite.

A drainpipe fastened to the side of the building caught his eye. It went up about six metres before becoming level with Ogilvie's window, but still about a metre and a half to the side of the window. However, it was his only hope, so "hand over hand up he went," the pipe creaking and shaking. He made it to the top and with great athleticism managed to swing a leg over to the window sill. Using the Venetian blinds, he swung into the room. Ogilvie remained sound asleep

Toronto Murders

throughout this ordeal until Capreol gently shook him. In a second, Capreol found himself seized by the throat and being rushed towards the open window. When Ogilvie realized who was in his grasp, he stood in astonishment, looking at his badly dishevelled and bleeding friend. On hearing the story, he quickly agreed to loan Capreol 21 sovereigns — more than enough for what was owing on the boat — and a change of clothes.

Meanwhile, George Kingsmill, the high bailiff (constable) of Toronto, had been out on the streets and noticed Capreol's odd behaviour. He followed him to the dock, and when he realized the steamer was leaving in the middle of the night, he tried to leap aboard. Kingsmill landed in the water instead and was helped onto the deck by Capreol. On being told where they were headed and what Capreol intended to do, Kingsmill demanded to be returned to shore. The captain refused, so Kingsmill had to go with them. He had no arrest warrants and did not think they would actually find the suspects.

Capreol's instincts could not have been better. When they reached Lewiston and went to a nearby tavern, lo and behold James and Grace were there, booked into different rooms.

Kingsmill arrested Grace easily and handed her to someone else to guard. He then woke James on the pretence of charging him with not paying duty on a horse. As soon as the fugitive heard that Kingsmill was a policeman from Toronto — and even though the subject of murder had not

He Said, She Said

come up — James blurted out, "I know all about it. Is there any reward offered for Nancy? If you find her you will know the whole secret. You may thank her for it all."

What James didn't know was that a few hours later Nancy's body would also be found in Kinnear's cellar. By the time the little group of captors and captives had returned to Toronto, James's attempt to blame Nancy was unhinged by the gruesome discovery. At the request of the coroner, the Kinnear house had been thoroughly searched. In a second room in the cellar, behind some empty wine casks and under an old wash tub, was Nancy's body, doubled up and starting to decompose. An autopsy later showed she was pregnant.

* * *

When she first appeared in court on August 3, 1843, Grace "was decently dressed, with a parasol in her hand, and seemed to have been collected enough to make her toilet with care," according to the *British Colonist*. It was quickly proven that everything she was wearing belonged to Nancy, just as most of James's attire belonged to Kinnear. The largest reaction from the spectators came when Grace announced she was just 16 years old.

Grace told the court that she did not even know Nancy had been murdered until she and James returned to Toronto, and that while she heard the shot that killed Kinnear, she did not help dispose of the body. Then why, the court asked, had she gone along with James's plan? And why did she not tell anyone what happened the first chance she got? Grace said it was fear; she was terrified of James.

> *Question:* "Why did you not disclose what had happened? Surely when you were on board the steamer, you need not have been frightened. If you had told Captain Richardson [on the way to the United States], you would have been protected and in a very different position now — if what you stated is true."
>
> *Grace:* "I could not get an opportunity; James stuck so close to me."
>
> *Question:* "Did not McDermott leave you at the City Hotel and go to get shaved?"
>
> *Grace:* "Yes."
>
> *Question:* "Well, when you were alone then, and need not have feared him — why did you not *then* give information?"
>
> *Grace:* "I was taking care of the horse and waggon [*sic*]."

A number of witnesses were presented to show that, besides the clothes the two accused were wearing, the horse, wagon, and many other of their possessions had been

He Said, She Said

Kinnear's. After five hours, it was decided that James and Grace would be held over for trial.

The trial began on November 3, 1843, with the two being tried only for the Kinnear murder. The lawyer for the defendants, Kenneth McKenzie, asked that they be tried separately. This was granted and the trial for James proceeded. It continued all day and far into the evening. As was common then, James stood for the whole day. The jury only took 10 minutes before returning with the verdict of guilty. At 1:30 a.m. the judge pronounced the death sentence.

Grace's trial took place the following day. It involved many of the same witnesses and, in the end, had the same outcome: she, too, was found guilty of murder and sentenced to death. The joint execution was scheduled for less than three weeks later. On hearing her sentence, Grace fainted — but apparently recovered quickly.

Appeals were launched immediately, though much more effort was made to save Grace's life than James's. On November 13, 1843, the warden at the Provincial Penitentiary received a letter from the governor general. It said in part, "His Excellency in Council has been pleased to direct that the sentence of death pronounced on James McDermott for the murder of Thomas Kinnear be allowed to take effect at the time and place appointed, and that the sentence pronounced on Grace Marks for the same crime be commuted into imprisonment in the Provincial Penitentiary at hard labour for the term of her natural life."

Toronto Murders

On November 21, 1843, James was hanged and Grace was taken to prison.

Capreol, without whom the two might never have been tracked down and arrested, went on to be the founder and chief organizer of the Northern Railway, extending from Toronto to Lake Huron. He never was repaid for his personal expenses in capturing the fugitives. (Said *Robertson's Landmarks of Toronto* about Capreol's efforts: "As a piece of detective work and executive ability it has never been approached by a civilian, and it is doubtful whether it has ever been equalled in sagacity, directness, triumph over obstacles and expeditious execution by any professional detective or officer.")

The press lambasted the officials who they considered had almost let the killers slip through their hands. "The delay occasioned by some of the magistrates objecting to incur the responsibility of chartering the steamer to go in quest of the prisoners, might have been of serious consequence," an editorial in the *British Colonist* stated. "It is to be hoped that in future, our authorities will allow their minds to expand a little more."

* * *

But Grace's story does not end there. She became a celebrity of sorts in her time. People were intrigued by the young convicted killer. One of those people was author Susanna

He Said, She Said

Moodie. Moodie and her sister, Catharine Parr Traill, are two of Canada's best-known female writers of the 19th century. Both were established writers before immigrating to Canada from Scotland in 1832 with their husbands. Best known for her book *Roughing It in the Bush* (published in 1852), Moodie also wrote *Life in the Clearings* the following year. In the latter she described a visit she made to the Provincial Penitentiary in Kingston, wanting, she said, to "introduce my reader to the female inmates of this house of woe and crime." There were only 40 of them which, Moodie wrote, "speaks much for the superior moral training of the feebler sex." Her main goal "was to look at the celebrated murderess, Grace Marks, of whom I had heard a great deal, not only from the public papers, but from the gentleman who defended her upon her trial, and whose able pleading saved her from the gallows, on which her wretched accomplice closed his guilty career."

Moodie went on to write the story of the murder, a much fictionalized version of what actually happened. She did, however, give a clear picture of Grace.

"She is a middle-sized woman with a slight graceful figure," she wrote. "There is an air of hopeless melancholy in her face which is very painful to contemplate. Her complexion is fair, and must, before the touch of hopeless sorrow paled it, have been very brilliant. Her eyes are a bright blue, her hair auburn, and her face would be rather handsome were it not for the long curved chin, which gives, as it always does to most persons who have this facial defect, a cunning, cruel expression."

By the time of Moodie's visit, Grace had shown herself to be exceptionally competent and was often working in the house of the prison's governor. Shortly after, however, she was transferred to the Lunatic Asylum in Toronto. Whether she faked her episode of madness as a sympathy ploy or whether she really had a breakdown will never be known, but Moodie was anxious to visit the asylum and observe Grace in its environment

Moodie found Grace was housed in the worst section. "These [wards] were occupied by patients that were not in a state to allow visitors a nearer inspection than observing them through glass doors. The hands of all these women were secured in mufflers; some were dancing, others running to and fro at full speed, clapping their hands, and laughing and shouting with the most boisterous merriment. How dreadful is the laugh of madness!"

Then she spotted Grace.

"Among these raving maniacs I recognized the singular face of Grace Marks — no longer sad and despairing, but lighted up with the fire of insanity, and glowing with a hideous and fiend-like merriment. On perceiving that strangers were observing her, she fled shrieking away like a phantom into one of the side rooms."

Not long after that, Grace was deemed healthy again and was returned to the prison. Another 15 years passed.

He Said, She Said

There were still efforts to have her released from prison. A *Globe and Mail* article in 1871 stated the government was considering it. "She has suffered prison life now for a period of 28 years on the 19th November," the article stated. "[A]mple justice has been meted to her, and a prolonged incarceration can certainly not forward the interests of herself and justice."

Officials obviously agreed. On August 2, 1872, the warden at the prison received a pardon for Grace Marks. Five days later, after 28 years and 10 months, Grace was released. The warden and his daughter accompanied her to New York to a home provided for her. No more is known of her from this time although it was rumoured that she married. Grace would come into prominence again in 1996 when she became the central figure in Margaret Atwood's novel, *Alias Grace*.

* * *

In a confession the day before his hanging, James pointed the finger directly at Grace.

He said: "She said now was the time to kill the housekeeper, and Mr. Kinnear when he returns home, and I'll assist you and you are a coward if you don't do it. I will not say how Mr. Kinnear and Nancy Montgomery were killed, but *I should not have done it*, if I had not been urged to do so by Grace Marks. After Nancy Montgomery was put in the cellar, Grace

Toronto Murders

several times went down there, and she afterwards told me she had taken her purse from her pocket ... Grace Marks is wrong in stating she had no hand in the murder; she was the means from beginning to end."

She said: "We then commenced packing up all the valuable things we could find. We both went down into the cellar; Mr. Kinnear was lying on his back in the cellar; I held the candle; McDermott took the keys and some money from his pockets; nothing was said about Nancy; I did not see her, but I knew she was in the cellar, and about 11 o'clock McDermott harnessed the horse; we put the boxes in the wagon and then started off for Toronto; he said he would go to the States and marry me. I consented to go ... [Later] I told McDermott I would stop at Lewiston, and would not go any further; he said he would make me go with him."

In the end it became "he said, she said" so many times that the complete truth about what happened that fateful weekend in 1843 would be obscured forever. The only certainties were that Thomas Kinnear and Nancy Montgomery had met violent deaths — and only James McDermott and Grace Marks knew at whose hands.

Chapter 3
Mum's the Word

Clara Ford had already confessed to the detectives. On November 21, 1894, she stood in the prisoner's box in court and, with her head down, quietly but firmly said "guilty" when asked for her plea to the murder charge.

Astonishment rumbled through the spectators' gallery. It caught even the magistrate off guard because accused murderers were not allowed to plead guilty in those years. He simply fixed his gaze on her and waited. Her lawyer quickly jumped up and whispered something in Clara's ear. When asked for her plea a second time, she answered "not guilty."

This odd turn seemed a fitting end to an equally odd murder mystery that began six weeks earlier in Toronto's upscale residential Parkdale area, stretching out along Lake Ontario.

Toronto Murders

* * *

On October 6, Willie Westwood, a young teenager, was with two friends near the Parkdale Station (a street railway system). It was 5 p.m. when they were approached by a man about 25 years old, who, Willie later said, "wore a fedora hat and a shabby, dark suit of clothes and looked generally tough." He asked for directions to 28 Jameson Avenue but, when told, did not head in that way.

"I wonder what he wants our house for?" Willie said to his friends.

* * *

Later in the day, Frank Westwood, Willie's 18-year-old brother, was out with three of his friends. The evening was unusually mild and there were many young people walking along Jameson Avenue. The friends walked around the streets, smoking and laughing. One by one, they left for home. Frank finally said goodbye to the last fellow at 10:10 p.m. and returned to his own home, Lakeside Hall, his parents' house. His father, Benjamin Westwood, a prosperous fishing tackle manufacturer, had already gone to bed with a cold. His mother was still up, however, and the two talked for a while before heading upstairs at 10:50 p.m.

Moments later, Frank heard the doorbell ring and went back downstairs. He lit a gas jet at the back end of the hall,

Mum's the Word

Fire brigade in the Parkdale area, Toronto, 1888

opened the inner glass door to the vestibule and then the outer oak door. What exactly happened next has always been open to speculation. Most reports said a gun was fired as soon as the door was open. A bullet struck the young man on the right side, below the last rib, and then spiralled downward, ripping through his liver and lodging itself near his spinal column.

"Mother! Mother, I'm shot!" he called out.

Mrs. Westwood called for her husband and ran downstairs, finding Frank on the floor, leaning up against the door. She could still see the smoke and smell the powder from the gun. When Mr. Westwood arrived, he started to run outside.

"Oh, Ben, don't!" his wife cried. "They might shoot you." He quickly retrieved his revolver from a locked box and went out to the front steps. Not seeing anything suspicious, he nevertheless fired a single shot in the air.

"This was for the purpose of arousing the neighbours and police if they were in the neighbourhood and to indicate to anyone lurking about that we were in a position to protect ourselves," he told *The Globe and Mail.*

While Mrs. Westwood was on the phone calling the doctor, Frank dragged himself to his feet and walked upstairs. By this time blood was seeping through both his vest and his pink shirt. Willie Westwood had also heard the shot that he later described as sounding like glass breaking. When Frank walked into his brother's bedroom, Willie asked him what all the noise was about. Frank said he was shot and opened his vest "where the blood was coming through his clothing." Willie jumped out of bed and his brother fell into his arms.

In 15 minutes, two doctors and the police had converged on Lakeside Hall. It was evident that Frank was seriously wounded and little could be done. The damage was so extensive they did not even dare to try to remove the bullet. Detective Charles Slemin was the first to interview Frank, who gave his description of the killer but said he did not recognize the man. When Slemin questioned him about his lady friends, Frank appeared to get annoyed and exclaimed "Oh, you can't pump me!" He also begged the officer not to search his clothes. (As it happened, his clothes were later searched

Mum's the Word

anyway, but nothing was found of any relevance to the case.) The loss of blood made him very weak and, after this interview, Frank was allowed to rest through the night.

When Sunday morning dawned, Frank was questioned repeatedly about the shooting, because most people — especially his father — were having a hard time believing he did not know who did it.

> *Mr. Westwood:* "Do you know who shot you, Frank?"
>
> *Frank:* "No."
>
> *Mr. Westwood:* "Are you quite sure you don't know?"
>
> *Frank:* "Yes."

Mr. Westwood continued like this until Frank finally said, "Oh, father, *don't* ask me any more. I have answered that question before." But over the next three days, he would answer it many more times.

On Monday, October 10, Frank was questioned for the first time by City Crown Attorney Curry. The family, he later recalled, seemed reluctant to let him talk to Frank. During the interview, Frank described his assailant as being "a man of medium height with light moustache, wearing a dark suit of clothes and a fedora hat." Frank also told Curry that in fact the shot hadn't come immediately when he opened the door that fateful night: he and the killer had briefly struggled in the hall before the shot was fired. Pressed by Curry further on this point, Frank seemed to backtrack. He wouldn't repeat what he'd said, and the subject never came up again throughout the investigation.

Curry stated later that he didn't think Frank realized at that point that he was not going to live. By Tuesday morning, however, Frank did know his life was ebbing away. It was a busy day as many friends and family were asked by Frank to come and say goodbye to him. He told them "he died game" (bravely).

One of his friends later related the story of Frank disposing of his few earthly possessions. The dying youth directed his parents to give his ring to his older brother, Bert, (Charles) and his tools to Willie, and to divide his share in the boat between two of his friends. Curry was also asked to come because Frank had agreed to give what was then starkly called "an ante-mortem statement." Dr. Lynd, Detective Slemin, and Curry would be the only ones to hear the dying man's declaration.

"I, Frank Westwood, believing that I am about to die, desire to state the facts connected with my being shot," the statement began. He then relayed mostly facts already known about the events of the evening. He did add that he had previously had some trouble with a man named Gus Clarke and, while the assailant wasn't Gus, he looked somewhat like "a man who chummed with him."

Mum's the Word

During the statement Frank swore he would tell who had done the shooting if he knew, "because whoever did it would do it again." The feeling that he knew more than he was telling never completely faded and Frank himself added to the mystery by saying, with regard to the possible identity of the killer, "mum's the word."

After 74 hours of suffering, Frank Westwood died on Wednesday, October 10, from acute liver infection and internal bleeding. He was buried in Mount Pleasant Cemetery two days later, the same day the inquest into his death began. The inquest took place once a week over the course of many weeks. Very little new information was learned. The mystery man whom Willie and his friend had seen on the evening of the murder turned out to be a man delivering a piano to the Westwood house.

A disturbance caused by some "stonehookers" at the beginning of September was also closely looked at. In an age before the ready availability of concrete, a constant supply of building stone was in demand. Stonehookers were men who mined the shallow waters of Lake Ontario for blocks of shale, loading them onto small sail-powered vessels (also called stonehookers). By the mid-1800s, however, lakeside farmers were complaining that the stripping of stone was destabilizing their land, leading to erosion. The Ontario government eventually passed a law prohibiting stonehookers from taking stone within 15 metres of shore. One evening, Frank had seen one of these vessels close to the Westwood boathouse and he suspected some illegal work going on. He thought he recognized one of the two men aboard as an acquaintance, Gus Clarke. Frank called to his father up at the house. Westwood senior opened his bedroom window and fired two shots from his revolver in the air to scare the men away.

Although the police checked the incident out again in investigating its possible link to the murder, in the end they decided there was no connection.

Authorities also looked at what, in those days, was a common motive for murdering a young man: that he had taken liberties with a woman and her father had come gunning for him. However, it seemed Frank had no known girlfriends and all his friends vouched for his honour. Still, the belief persisted that he knew more than he was saying and had protected his family by keeping quiet.

* * *

Public interest waned as the inquest dragged on week after week and even the police had given up hope until Gus Clarke said something that piqued their interest. His testimony at the inquest was insignificant, but in talking to police afterwards he told them about a mulatto woman he knew of. She not only used to dress up in men's clothing, but had once lived at the end of the property adjacent to the Westwood house. Her name was Clara Ford. Gus said he had also heard

Mum's the Word

her threaten to "do in" young Westwood if she found him with another woman.

On November 20, 1894, police tracked down Clara Ford at the tailor's where she worked and lived in a room upstairs. According to their report, when they told her they wanted to take her in for questioning, she asked them if they could first go to her room. They agreed and, once there, asked Clara if she had any men's clothes. She freely admitted it and showed them a waistcoat, coat and trousers. When they asked Clara if she had a gun (which she did), she apparently got suspicious even though they had not yet told her why they wanted to talk to her.

"Oh, it's the Westwood case you're after," Clara was quoted as saying.

Clara was then taken to the police station and questioned for eight hours straight. Finally, it was said, she gave in.

"It is no use misleading you any longer in the matter," Clara was said to have told Detective Henry Reburn, who cautioned her before she went on. "I don't care. I deserve what I'll get, but if you had had a sister treated like that you would do the same thing." When Reburn asked what she meant, Clara replied, "I shot Frank Westwood." Her motive was simple.

"At the end of July or the end of August, he caught hold of me at the foot of Jameson Avenue and tried to knock me down and take improper liberties with me. I promised to get even with him then." But she added that she had not intended to kill him.

Toronto Murders

When it was announced that Clara had been arrested, news of her confession was kept quiet for a few days. Frank's father was relieved at the prospect the mystery would be cleared up. "Of course, it will not give us back our boy, but it will give the lie to the dreadful insinuations which have been made in some of the papers ... against the family," Westwood told *The Globe and Mail*. But his assumption that the arrest would silence the rumours of an indiscretion on Frank's part was wrong. When Clara's confession was released, it pointed the finger at Frank for taking advantage of her.

When Clara was brought into court on November 21, 1894, to hear the charge of murder read against her, *The Globe and Mail* wrote of her:

"She was neatly dressed in a dark skirt, vest bodice and fur-trimmed cloak, a stand up collar and tie, and a black fedora hat trimmed with ribbon and a feather. Her hair was short and close curled to her head, and her features showing clearly her Negro blood."

Following her "guilty" and then "not guilty" pleas, Clara was returned to prison until the preliminary hearing on November 28. Her arrest for Frank's murder triggered a great deal of interest again in the public — and the press. Before Clara's arrest, the *Toronto World* had sent their articles on the murder to Arthur Conan Doyle, creator of Sherlock Holmes. He was due in Toronto on November 26 and the paper decided it would be interesting to see if he could solve the murder. On his arrival, he said he had read all the articles with interest and called it "a strangely absorbing mystery." He was not impressed, however, with how Clara's confession was obtained.

"As to the present prisoner, Clara Ford, I cannot offer an opinion; I have never met with such a case as hers," he told the *Toronto World*. "The system of closeting a prisoner with an officer and cross-questioning her for hours savors more of French than English methods of justice."

Before the confession was read to the court, rumours were running rampant as to the motive for the murder and to the nature of Clara herself. She was 33 years old and the night of the murder was not the first time she had worn men's clothing. The *Toronto World* figured it had the answer as to motive and explained it to their readers:

"There is considerable reason for believing that this young woman is a sufferer from what the medical authorities call homo-sexuality [*sic*], in other words that she was suffering from what is called sexual perversion. Such women go about in male clothing. They prefer masculine work and show an unusual skill in it. They eschew female occupations and often show a weakness for smoking and spirits. With this perverted condition there often go pronounced outbreaks of passion and jealousy which drive the unfortunate victim to crime."

The paper had a medical man theorize that if Frank had "interfered" with Clara as she masqueraded as a man, threatening to expose her and "rob her of her pleasure," it would be enough to provoke an attack. Also, added the paper, another characteristic of "these creatures" is that "they revel in blood."

Clara's true story would be much more complicated. As a young black woman, her mother had gone to work as a maid for a well-to-do Toronto family. She became pregnant by her employer's son and was promptly fired. Clara was the result of this liaison and when she was a few days old, her mother left her on the family's doorstep. At the end of their property lived a washerwoman, Miss McKay, to whom the family gave a sum of money to take Clara and raise her. When the money ran out, Miss McKay placed the girl in a home, but was persuaded by her brother to bring the child back, saying he would help with support. He eventually died, but by that time Miss McKay and Clara were close, and the woman kept the girl and took her along from one high-standing family to another on her rounds as a laundress. From the time Clara was 12 years old, she was supporting herself and learned to become a good tailoress. She continued to live with Miss McKay and, by all accounts, was very good to the woman who had raised her.

Clara moved to Chicago, for a time, but finding work there for a "black girl" was impossible. The only work available was as a prostitute. This was not for Clara, so she purchased some boys' clothing and, dressed as a young man, had no trouble finding work at a stable. During her time in Chicago, Clara was also married and had two small children. Both had apparently died.

Mum's the Word

* * *

Clara's confession was read to the court at her preliminary hearing on November 28, 1894. The court heard that Clara had at first said she was at the theatre the night of the murder, with Florence McKay, 14, another girl raised by Miss McKay. When the police brought Florence in, however, the young woman said that Clara had not shown up at the theatre. At that point, Clara's own motive for the murder as a "wronged woman" was publicized. *The Globe and Mail* printed an article saying it believed both the confession and the motive Clara gave for committing the murder, because it made sense to them. The *Toronto World* — which had so quickly labelled Clara a sexual pervert — was incensed by this. It was quite right to believe the confession, the paper said but it was outrageous that *The Globe and Mail* so readily accepted the woman's motive, which could so easily damage the reputation of such a fine, upstanding family!

Because of her confession, it was a foregone conclusion of the preliminary hearing that Clara would be held over for trial. "So terrible and minute a confession has seldom if ever been heard in a Canadian court of justice," *The Globe and Mail* reported. The trial was postponed to the April 1895 assizes in Toronto and her supporters did not waste the intervening months. Clara already had W.G. Murdoch as her lawyer, but one of the top criminal lawyers in the city was also acquired to lead her defence, E.F.B. "Blakie" Johnston. One of his trademarks was that he did not talk to his client. He would have all the facts of the case given to him and then he would lay out a defence strategy and stick with it.

And strategy became the whole key in defending Clara Ford against a murder charge, especially in light of her confession.

The trial began on April 30, 1895, in front of Chancellor John Boyd. Representing the Crown was B.B. Osler, as he had done in so many other famous cases (including the successful prosecution of Louis Riel). During the prosecution portion of the Clara Ford trial, Osler's wife died suddenly and he handed over the prosecution to Hartley Dewart. The change made little difference because Osler had already presented damning evidence against Clara for three days. She was, he said, known to dress in men's clothing. She owned a gun that was the same calibre as the murder weapon. She had once lived very near the Westwood house and so knew the neighbourhood well. She was overheard threatening Frank's life. And — most significantly — she had confessed to the crime.

In his opening address, Osler acknowledged there had obviously been a relationship between Westwood and Clara. "Westwood's story is the old one of love and passion ... It is the story of a mulatto girl who had been the plaything of an apparently respectable young man," he told the court. "Discarded by him for another, she deliberately shot him to death."

Mum's the Word

The three days of testimony painted a crystal clear picture of Clara as a killer with means, motive, and opportunity. It left her lawyers with a seemingly insurmountable obstacle. Using the "wronged woman" defence would normally have been the way to go for Johnston, but this was problematic with Clara and her history. To see her in this light might have stretched credibility.

To make the motive reasonable, reported the *Toronto World*, "it must first be established that Clara Ford was a virtuous young woman, so virtuous in fact that she was shocked at the approaches of a boy fourteen years younger than herself; that she led a moral life and was extremely sensitive of her reputation for morality." The article concluded, "The evidence so far does not establish this fact."

Johnston obviously agreed. His first major move was on May 2 when the Crown brought Clara's confession into the record. Johnston tried to have the confession thrown out of court, but he was unsuccessful. The following day, the Crown closed its portion of the trial in the morning.

Short of options, Johnston stunned the entire courtroom when the court reconvened after lunch.

"We call the prisoner, my Lord," he said to Judge Boyd.

Female witnesses in trials were not uncommon, but a female prisoner — especially one on trial for her life — had never been put on the stand before. Johnston had decided to make Clara a female victim after all, but at the hands of overly aggressive policemen who forced her to confess to something she did not do. Murdoch did the questioning and, as he began, Clara "leant over the front of the dock," asking her lawyer to speak louder because she was deaf. She then began to tell her version of the day she was arrested. She was working at Barnett's tailor shop when Detectives Slemin and Porter came in. They did not identify themselves as policemen, or say they were there to talk to her. While Porter engaged her in small talk, Slemin took the owner of the shop outside to talk before returning.

"We want to see your room," Slemin said to Clara when he came back in, but still didn't identify himself.

"I says 'What d'ye want to see my room for?' and he says 'Well, we want to see it.' So I put the iron down and went up the stairs and Slemin followed with Porter behind him."

When they entered her room, Slemin closed the door behind them and asked her if she had any men's clothing. "By that time I had a suspicion they were detectives. I hesitated a minute because I wondered who had told them about the men's clothes and then he asked me again and I said 'Yes.'"

No, she told them, she had not gone to Parkdale disguised as an old man or woman and, no, she did not have a moustache. When asked by the men if she had a revolver, she replied she did "and then it struck me all in a flash that it was the Westwood tragedy."

They told Clara that Detective Stark wanted to see her at the police station. She had no idea she was under arrest. At the station, Clara was questioned by Inspector Reburn who

Mum's the Word

tried to get her to admit she had been in Parkdale the night of the murder. Stark came in and attacked her wearing of men's clothes, but did not get very far.

"He says 'What were you doing wearing men's clothes?' I says 'I don't know that it's any harm to wear men's clothes.' He says 'Don't you know it's against the law?' 'Well, if it is,' I says, 'how about Vic Steinberg, who goes to a baseball match in Hamilton in men's clothes and then writes it all up in *The News*?' He didn't say any more."

Clara told them that the night of the killing she had been at the theatre with Florence McKay. She stuck with that even when they produced the young girl who said Clara never showed up. In court, Clara never wavered from that story and talked of how the two of them walked along Adelaide to Yonge Street and then to Queen Street and westbound from there.

The questioning at the police station had continued and Clara told her interrogators that she had not worn her men's clothes in almost a year and had given the hat away. Finally, when the detectives presented her with the information that Florence denied they went to the theatre, Clara told them the girl was lying. At that, Reburn had taken Clara into another gas-lit room, shut the door and the windows, and drew down the blinds.

"'Clara,' he threatened, "'if you don't tell this it'll be the worse for you. If you were my own sister I couldn't do more for you.' I said I didn't know anything about it. Then he said 'Only tell me what your motive was. Say that he insulted

Yonge Street looking north from Queen Street, Toronto, 1890

you ... if you tell me all I won't say a word about it and I'll see that you're a free woman and walk the streets again.'" In the end, she said, she got confused and believed them, and then confessed.

In court, Clara spent 2 hours and 10 minutes telling her story of the interrogation. She spent another hour and 10 minutes being cross-examined, not flinching once, and giving straight and direct answers to all questions.

"All who saw the girl stand in that witness box for three

Mum's the Word

hours answering her own counsel or fencing with the Crown could not but admire her wonderful nerve," *The Globe and Mail* wrote of her testimony.

When the trial resumed the next morning, three men from *The Evening Telegram* testified they followed the route that the detectives claimed Clara took the evening of the murder and it was not possible to follow it. Two witnesses from the theatre swore she had been at the theatre that night, but they could not be sure if anyone was with her.

At 2:55 p.m., Johnston began his address to the jury. He continued for 2 hours and 17 minutes. He pointed out that he and Murdoch were not being paid a cent for this case; they took it only because they believed their client to be innocent.

He also attacked the detectives for their merciless "digging" at his client for eight hours and "was it any wonder that she, womanlike, would say anything to get out of the clutches of those vultures? The action of the prisoner in going into the witness box with her life in her hands and, with all the charm and confidence of innocence, telling her story, was one of the boldest, noblest, most heroic acts ever witnessed in a criminal court in this land. Had she been guilty she would not have dared to do it."

Prosecutor Dewart's closing address to the jury followed and even he gave grudging respect to Clara's appearance in the box, but said it did not change the facts of the case. He spoke for more than an hour and was followed by the magistrate whose remarks to the jury were decidedly against Clara.

Toronto Murders

Because of this, when the jury retired at 8:45 p.m., most in the courtroom expected it to be a long night or a quick conviction. They got neither. The jury returned to the courtroom within an hour. When the "not guilty" verdict was read out, a loud cheer erupted in the courtroom. Clara thanked the crowd and said, "This does the boys of Toronto credit."

* * *

The case of Clara Ford made her somewhat of a celebrity. A play about the murder, *The Séance of Lakeside Hall*, was published in 1990. In 1943, an issue of a true crime magazine, *Daring Crime*, featured "The Case of Clara Ford" — and asserted that she got away with murder.

Reports in the papers after her trial said Clara occasionally dressed in men's clothing and appeared in some questionable dime museum exhibitions around the subject of the murder. Her lawyer, Johnston, was outraged by this and recommended she leave town. Whether these accounts were true or not, it is known is that in September 1895 she appeared as one of "Creoles" in the Sam T. Jack Company performing in a theatre in Buffalo, New York. The group later appeared in Toronto.

Did Clara Ford shoot Frank Westwood? Perhaps Frank said it best in the last few days of his life: mum's the word.

Chapter 4
Murder and Bigotry

 locked door. A man slumped over a desk, his arms and face burned by fire. A tin of coal oil. A bullet hole in the man's head. No gun.

The makings of a Sherlock Holmes mystery? No: Samuel Goldberg was a very real victim in this 1930 murder.

* * *

The fire alarm at the corner of Dundas and McCaul streets in Toronto was pulled at 6:45 p.m. on March 5, 1931. A few minutes later, two "hose wagons" arrived together at the Goldberg Monument Works at 153 St. Patrick Street, and firemen James Stevens and Charles England rushed to a side door in the building. The door was locked, but they could see smoke seeping from the structure and the faint glow of a flame inside. England forced open the door and a dozen firemen raced into the building. In the dark, they easily found the fire in the office section of the one-storey building and, in the dark, could see flames flickering around what turned out to be a desk. The first shot of water extinguished the flames and left the men unable to see in the smoky interior.

Fireman James Ridout moved towards the desk and began groping around until his hand touched a head. He called for a light and an "electric torch" was flashed on the desk. The fire call took a gruesome turn with the discovery of a body.

"His head had dropped forward on to the desk and his arms were about his face," *The Globe and Mail* reported. "The fire, apparently, had been centred about his body, since his face, head and hands were badly burned, while the desk was only partially destroyed and the wall behind him was barely charred. The remains of a fur-lined overcoat rested about him."

The man's watch had stopped at 6:04 p.m.

Detective Fred Storm arrived on the scene at 6:50 p.m. and testified at the subsequent inquest that the face was so badly burned when he saw it that "it looked like a roast of pork." Just after 7 p.m., he left the building in search of Abraham Steinberg, a partner in the business who he knew lived nearby. Storm didn't have far to go because Abraham

Murder and Bigotry

had just joined the crowd gathered outside the building. Taking him to the scene of the fire, Storm asked him if he could identify the body in the chair.

"It's Sam," Abraham replied.

Storm asked him, "How can you tell by that face it's Sam?"

"Sure, it's Sam," Abraham answered, "He's a big man."

Sam Goldberg, 35, was one of four partners in the business that supplied tombstones for those buried in Jewish cemeteries. His partners were his three uncles, Abraham Steinberg and Harry and Abraham Goldberg.

Chief Coroner Malcolm Crawford arrived at 7:10 p.m. and had the body removed to the morgue. It was Dr. Burr, performing the autopsy, who found the true cause of death. It was assumed up to this point that Goldberg had died from the effects of the fire. However, Burr discovered a bullet hole in Sam's head. The bullet had entered Goldberg's head 10.2 centimetres above the right ear, and had emerged 6.4 centimetres above the left ear. According to Burr, the shot had been fired by someone standing above Sam, who would have been sitting at his desk at the time. After being shot, Sam's clothing and the upper part of his body were covered with coal oil and set ablaze — presumably to cover up the murder.

The police began to focus their attention on Abraham Steinberg, in spite of the fact he had an alibi for the time of the murder. A stonemason by trade, Abraham had been born in Russia in 1880. He spoke English with difficulty and had a strong accent. He was a short man of about 5 feet, 3 inches, with blue eyes, dark brown hair, and false teeth. On March 6, 1930, he appeared in court on a charge of vagrancy and was remanded in custody, bail being denied. (Vagrancy was a charge once used to hold people who were suspected of committing a serious crime, but could not be charged because of a lack of evidence. During the three days they were held "for vagrancy," it was hoped that enough evidence would be found to warrant an upgrade in the charges.)

Two days after the murder, detectives searched the monument works premises for a weapon and a bullet. One of them discovered a revolver under a pile of cement sacks. According to police, one of the shells had been discharged. Then, on the same day, in another search of the office, the detectives happened to pick up a piece of partly burned charcoal. One of them said that when he crumbled it, a bullet dropped to the floor. The police felt they had established that the revolver belonged to Abraham, but sent the gun and bullet to a gun expert in Montreal, Dr. Wilfred Derome, to determine if it was the actual murder weapon. As soon as the telegram from Derome arrived on March 24 confirming that this was the case, the police arrested Abraham Steinberg and charged him with the murder of his nephew.

The inquest into Sam Goldberg's murder took place on April 8, 1930. The jury heard evidence of Abraham's ownership of the revolver found on the property, and heard from a witness who saw a man dressed in a grey coat and hat going

Murder and Bigotry

into the business at 5:30 p.m. on the evening of the murder. The man appeared to take a key out of his pocket and open the door. Evidence that Sam and Abraham had been feuding for the previous few months was also brought forward. Despite additional testimony on Abraham's behalf, in the end the Coroner's jury stated that "we are unanimously of the opinion that the said Abraham Steinberg had knowledge of the crime."

* * *

The trial began on October 6, 1930, with I.F. Hellmuth and T.H. Lennox defending Abraham. The prosecution's case, led by Crown Prosecutor J.C. Makins, started by showing that there were only four keys to Goldberg Monumental Works. Sam's key was with him, Harry Goldberg was out of town, and Abraham Goldberg had not been near the building that day. The prosecutors also proved the murder weapon had belonged to Abraham, though they couldn't prove that he was the one who actually used the gun in question to kill Sam. And, try as they might, they were unable to prove that Abraham even owned a grey coat and hat, let alone was wearing it that night. All the witnesses on his behalf stated he was wearing a blue coat and hat that day.

Harry Goldberg told the trial of an incident two months earlier that led to the antagonism between Abraham and Sam. The four owners were considering bringing in a fifth

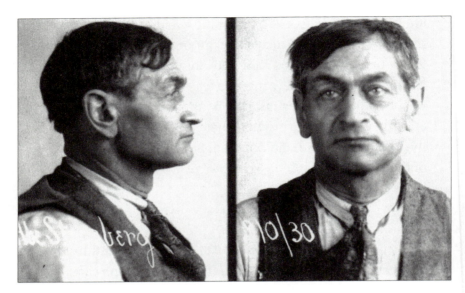

Abraham Steinberg

partner, Nathan Chapnick. Abraham, it was said, was not really happy about it and had told Chapnick they were all only making $17 a week. Sam, however, had said that was not true — that they were earning $38 a week. "They got sore at each other" Harry Goldberg testified, "and Abraham called Steinberg a *puer*."

When Judge Nicol Jeffrey asked the witness the meaning of *puer*, Goldberg replied that it meant "a farmer, or a fellow who was not well educated." (In reality, *puer* is dog excrement — something Judge Jeffrey probably didn't know.) That was the only time, Goldberg said, that Sam had been

Murder and Bigotry

"rude and unkind" to Abraham. But from then on, the two did not speak unless it was "very necessary in their work." Harry Goldberg also testified that Abraham wanted to know how the business was being conducted and asked for an audit to be conducted. The audit, which Abraham paid for himself, showed that he actually owed the business $328. And a month before the murder, Abraham had said he was going to give six months' notice to leave the business. On cross-examination by defence lawyer Hellmuth, Goldberg acknowledged that Abraham had willingly paid both for the cost of the audit and the $328 owing.

Joseph Csuhaj, a Hungarian who testified through an interpreter, was the only witness who most likely saw the killer. At the time of the murder, he had been living on St. Patrick Street and his window faced the Goldbergs' shop. He told the court he saw a man entering the building between 5:30 and 6:00 p.m. on the night of the fire, but could not tell what direction he had come from.

"How was the man dressed?" Makins asked him.

"He had on a grey overcoat and a grey cap," Csuhaj replied. He also stated that the man was 2 inches taller than someone he pointed to in the court who was the same height as himself (Csuhaj was 5 feet 2 inches tall). This discrepancy between the height of the intruder and Abraham was raised by the defence many times. Csuhaj also told the court the man took what appeared to be a key out of his pocket and used it to open the door. The defence responded with the fact that when one of the partners was in the building, that door was always unlocked and if the man in question was Abraham he would have known this and not used the key.

The most important of the prosecution witnesses was James Creighton, a man who was in jail (charged with forgery) when he reportedly had a conversation with Abraham Steinberg. Creighton testified that during that conversation, Abraham had confessed to the murder. He allegedly told Creighton that, on the day of the murder, he had gone down to work and had taken the gun with him for protection because of an argument he'd had with his nephew. According to Creighton, Abraham had asked Sam what he was going to do about giving him a settlement when he left the business. Sam had told him he'd be thrown out. At that point, Abraham pulled his gun and it went off accidentally. In Creighton's version, Abraham then set fire to everything, threw the gun out behind the building, and went to a nearby store.

Defence lawyer Lennox was quick to point out that Creighton had told two different stories of the confession to two separate policemen. And the other defence lawyer, Hellmuth, told the court they could "not hang a dog on the story" told by Creighton.

Also presented by the prosecution was a pair of overalls that had been seized from Abraham's house. They were clean, but the spots on them, said the prosecutors, looked like blood stains. No evidence was produced to show that the blood belonged to Sam or even that it was human blood.

Murder and Bigotry

When the defence began its case, it focused largely on Abraham's alibi. At 5:15 on the evening of the murder, Abraham had entered Max Rotenberg's wholesale clothing store at 175 Dundas Street. The two knew each other well and Abraham was often in the store. Rotenberg testified that Abraham stayed at the store until 7 p.m. Four other customers in the store verified the testimony. Rotenberg also swore that Abraham was wearing a blue overcoat that day. Abraham's wife, Ida (described in *The Globe and Mail* as "a frail, poorly dressed woman"), testified that her husband never wore overalls to work.

The trial and summations ended at 4:45 p.m. on October 10 and the jury retired, reappearing at Judge Jeffrey's request shortly after 8 p.m. He asked if there was any chance of them reaching a conclusion. "I do not think so, my lord," said a jury member. The judge asked them to try and they again retired. At 8:47 p.m. they reappeared, deadlocked.

"I regret I have to accept your decision," Judge Jeffrey stated. "In view of the jury's disagreement, nothing remains but to remand the accused in custody for further trial."

Abraham, who had been crying intermittently throughout the day, had tears of joy in his eyes when he heard the result of the jury's deliberation. He assumed he would be freed. When he heard the judge's decision he realized he was wrong.

His second trial opened February 2, 1931. Abraham

was again defended by Hellmuth and Lennox. Judge Jeffrey presided as before.

The prosecution, led this time by Charles Bell, wasted no time in filling in one of the holes they felt had been in the evidence presented at the first trial. All the witnesses who had seen Abraham at Rotenberg's the evening of the murder swore he was wearing a blue overcoat and hat. The Crown suddenly produced a new witness, Sergeant Lou Williams, who testified that when Abraham was taken to detective headquarters on the night of the murder he had on a grey overcoat and cap. In the defence's cross-examination, Hellmuth asked Williams whether or not he had discussed the case with any other detectives. Williams replied that he had. Hellmuth then asked if he had known that the question of the colour of the overcoat had been raised at the former trial. At this point, Judge Jeffrey requested the jury to retire. He asked the lawyers that references to the former trial be avoided, and suggested the phrase "on another occasion" be used.

"But that is the very trouble," Hellmuth replied. "This witness [Williams] never testified at the first trial. I am going to challenge the bona-fide character of his evidence." Hellmuth was allowed to continue, but was not able to elicit anything from the detective to help the defence.

The prosecution also produced further evidence regarding the discovery at Abraham's home of the stained overalls. When the witness, Detective Levitt, was asked if the spots on the overalls looked like anything in particular, he replied,

Murder and Bigotry

"They looked like blood." Hellmuth immediately objected and the judge said he did not think the witness could say they looked like blood. Levitt then rephrased his answer, saying they were "dark spots of a red colour."

Before the next day's proceedings began, a sensational story began spreading, aided by a *Globe and Mail* article headlined "'Taken for a Ride' If He Gives Evidence, Witness Is Warned." James Creighton, the Crown's star witness in the first trial, reportedly had had a couple of visitors at his home the previous evening.

"Two thugs, one of whom is alleged to have flashed a revolver to confirm his statements, gained entrance to the home of James Creighton Monday night," the article stated. After feeding him "doped liquor," the story went on, they threatened to "take him for a ride" if he did not change his story at the trial. The two intruders were said to have posed as insurance agents to gain entry, and then had shared wine with Creighton before revealing their real reason for being there. After they left, Creighton became sick and was convinced they poisoned the liquor to prevent him from testifying. Officials did not confirm the story, but he was given protection and moved from his home.

The defence lawyers cross-examined Creighton extensively. He said that the first time he met and talked with Abraham, the accused hadn't said anything about his case, telling Creighton he was under orders from his lawyers not to talk to anyone. Yet, according to Creighton, the next time the two met in the hallway, Abraham — coming from another visit with his lawyers — had suddenly confessed the entire story of the murder to him. The defence questioned the credibility of this.

"Here is a man charged with murder who told you that his lawyer warned him not to talk to anybody," Lennox said to Creighton, "and immediately after leaving his lawyer he discloses this story. That is correct, is it?"

"He told me the story," Creighton replied.

"I say immediately after coming up from seeing his lawyers?"

"That is correct," Creighton answered.

But when Lennox and Hellmuth also tried to tell the court about Creighton's shady dealings in the past, Judge Jeffrey stopped them.

The Crown then produced another surprise witness, Wentworth Budd, another inmate of the jail. Hellmuth objected strenuously to this unscheduled witness, but was overruled by the judge and Budd was allowed to testify. His story about what Abraham told him was different from Creighton's version. He said that Abraham and Sam had been quarrelling and that the day before the murder Abraham had brandished an unloaded revolver at Sam. After another argument the next day, Abraham left the shop at 5:30 p.m. When he went back a few minutes later, he claimed to have found Sam slumped over his desk, dead. Cross-examined by Lennox, Budd admitted to the court that he had been

Murder and Bigotry

convicted three times for fraud and for false pretences and that he was still in jail.

Sam's mother also testified for the prosecution, through an interpreter. She was estranged from Sam and had not spoken to him for three years. Nevertheless, she often visited Abraham and his wife and had been there two days before the murder. At the first trial, Mrs. Goldberg made no mention of Abraham wearing a grey overcoat that day, but that became her testimony at the second trial. When asked by Lennox why she had not mentioned the grey coat at the previous trial, the interpreter replied for her, "I did not think I needed to say it before."

> *Lawyer:* "What made you say it today?"
> *Mrs. Goldberg:* "I heard I had to say it."
> *Lawyer:* "Who told you to say it?"
> *Mrs. Goldberg:* "Nobody told me. I have ears. I heard Mrs. Steinberg say Steinberg did not have a grey coat."

Mrs. Goldberg also said that Abraham had told her of the "arguments" he had had with her son, and said that he was "suffering" as a result of them.

As it did in the first trial, the defence focused on the witnesses who all saw Abraham at Rotenberg's store during the time the murder took place — and who all said they saw him wearing a blue coat. Both Rotenberg and his wife testified this time around, as did two customers with no direct connection to the store or Abraham Steinberg.

After the summations, the jury prepared to leave the courtroom to begin their deliberations — but not before Hellmuth voiced strong objection to the charge Jeffrey had given them.

"The attitude your lordship took is entirely one-sided," Hellmuth stated, adding that the evidence of the defence had not been presented in "anything like the same manner" as the evidence of the Crown had been presented. He pointed especially to the fact that Jeffrey had not alluded at all to the evidence that Harry Goldberg, another partner in the firm, and Peter Stewart, an employee, had both sworn they had never seen Abraham wear anything but a blue overcoat. Hellmuth was also upset that Jeffrey had put forward his own theory in connection with the alibi evidence, suggesting that it was perhaps "too pat." Hellmuth even went so far as to say the Judge's charge had been "hostile" to the accused, at which point Jeffrey declared, "I resent any such statement." Nevertheless, he did recall the jury to give them further instructions on some of his omissions.

In three and a half hours, the jury returned with a verdict of guilty. Abraham's shoulders slumped and he turned to stare at them in disbelief. When the court clerk repeated the verdict, he bowed his shaking head as his eyes filled with tears. He was sentenced to hang on April 21, 1931.

Murder and Bigotry

But the case was not quite closed yet. A fight to save Abraham from the gallows began.

Lennox and Hellmuth appealed the sentence to the Supreme Courts of Ontario and Canada, but faced an uphill battle, thanks in large part to Judge Jeffrey. It was customary for the judge overseeing the trial to write a summary of the trial and its findings and verdict to the federal minister of justice, in this case Hugh Guthrie. Most summaries were just that, a summary of the Crown and defence cases. However, in his report to Guthrie, Jeffrey was anything but balanced, stating he believed Abraham to be guilty. "To my mind the evidence given for the accused was not impressive," he wrote. "I have no doubt myself as to Steinberg's guilt; and it was a cold-blooded murder." He did acknowledge that "it is true that the evidence of Creighton and Budd must have greatly influenced the Jury."

Jeffrey ended his report saying, "If my opinion should be asked, I can say I can see no reason why the death sentence should not be carried out." Guthrie was the one who would make any decision on clemency, and this report was clearly not about to help Abraham's cause.

However, because of the appeals, the date of execution was postponed to July 14. Both appeals were for a new trial, but the guilty verdict was upheld in both cases, although not by a majority. Chief Justice William Mullock even went on record as saying that "the summing up of the trial judge was not fair to the accused, and may have caused a miscarriage of justice."

Toronto Murders

Abraham tried to hold out hope, but knew the chances were slim. He said so in a long letter to his wife, translated into English by his spiritual advisor, Rabbi Samuel Sachs. It said in part:

> *My beloved wife:*
> *Though I know full well that you feel with me the pain that I am suffering here behind the bars of death, still I feel that I must express in words some of my experiences in order to relieve somewhat the burden that is pressing on my heart ... Here, on the threshold of death, my blood seems to coagulate and agonizing thoughts come knocking at the windows of my mind. Oh, the ticking away of my last hours, the rushing of the precious minutes in the race of death! And the last minute coming to extinguish the spark of life and leave an undeserved stain on my name. But I am comforted in the knowledge that you, my dearest, feel my pain and know my innocence which, I still hope, will some day be proven. Adieu my dearest. ABRAHAM.*

Petitions with 40,000 signatures were circulated and then delivered to Minister of Justice Hugh Guthrie. They pointed to the many doubts in Abraham's guilt, especially surrounding the grey coat, his alibi, and the apparent discrepancy between his height and that of the intruder (reported

Murder and Bigotry

by the witness Csuhaj). Letters from Rabbi Sachs and from Abraham's 15-year-old daughter, Ida, were also sent to Guthrie. "He [Abraham] has never, directly or by intimation, said or hinted at anything that might make me suspect his guilt of the crime for which he has been convicted, or make me doubt his innocence," Sachs wrote. Ida begged for her father's life.

It was all to no avail. Guthrie and members of the Cabinet decided they would not make a recommendation to the governor general to commute the sentence. Abraham, informed of this by Sachs on July 13 and knowing his fate was sealed, declared, "I did not kill Sam Goldberg, I do not know who killed him, nor do I know anything about his death."

His wife and children went to see him for the last time that day.

That evening as the family waited at home in the hope of some last-minute commutation of Abraham's death sentence, the telephone rang and Abraham's daughter answered it. An unidentified man said to her, "I have just arrived from Ottawa with the order commuting Abraham Steinberg's death sentence to one of imprisonment. I will be over in a few minutes."

They waited all night for his arrival. He never came. It had been a hoax.

* * *

Toronto Murders

Abraham's last hours were spent with Rabbi Sachs. "Christ was the first. The Jew was the second," Abraham repeated over and over as he walked from his cell to the gallows. "They hang the Jew for someone else." He stepped onto the gallows as Sachs continued the prayers. Just before the trap was sprung at 8:03 a.m., Abraham uttered his last words: "Go ahead, hang the Jew."

Chapter 5
My Brother's Keeper

John Coursey went straight past eccentric and into downright strange.

At times he appeared normal, but his future in-laws were horrified when he stayed overnight with them for the first time.

"He was put into a double bedded room. He had one bed and I had the other," his betrothed's brother, Edward Tucker, later recalled. "At first he commenced to pray. Then he launched forth into swearing, then singing. He kept that up continually through the night until the morning. That was my first introduction to [him]."

Things did not improve when he set up home in Creemore, Ontario, in spite of a seemingly stable marriage and family, which included the birth of three sons over the course of five years.

"When he came to our house at the time, the Prince of Wales was in Toronto [September 1860]," Tucker continued. "He came in and sat down in the centre of the room. He then started and made all kinds of faces. That lasted for perhaps 15 or 20 minutes ... Then he asked for cold potatoes. This lasted another 15 or 20 minutes. Then he got up, as reasonable and rational as any other man."

What was he like to visit in his own home? "I have seen him put a buffalo skin on him and instead of going to bed as a reasonable man would, he would lay down on the roadside and stay there until morning," Tucker said.

Coursey moved his family to Lambton Mills in 1857 when his first son, Robert, was two years old. Lambton Mills was a thriving village of 500 people, situated at the crossing of the Humber River and Dundas Street West. The lives of local villagers revolved around the three mills in the area. The longest surviving one was William Cooper's Grist and Saw Mill, built in 1806 on the east bank of the river. The settlement that grew up around it was originally known as Cooper's Mills, but in 1838, in honour of a visit by John George Lambton, first Earl of Durham, the name was changed to the Village of Lambton Mills. (In 1840, Cooper's Grist and Saw Mill was leased by William Pearce Howland, who went on to become the only American-born Father of Confederation and father to two future mayors of Toronto.)

My Brother's Keeper

When John Coursey moved into the community in 1857, he purchased a house near one of the toll gates set up along Dundas Street. He ran the toll gate and also opened the De Coursier Hotel, changing the family name in the process.

Toll gates were set up in the 1800s throughout the Toronto region for much the same reason as they exist today: to pull in revenue to pay for road works. The operation of the toll gates was leased out to individuals. This arrangement was never very successful, however, because fights often erupted between the users and those running the gates.

The De Coursier Hotel and toll gate came to be well-known in the region, as did John's eccentric behaviour.

"He was a kind of curious being always," Samuel Bryans would later remember. Bryans had been a boyhood friend of Robert. "He would hitch up a rig and drive around harum-scarum like, as if he did not know where he was going. He would go through the village backwards and forwards. He did not seem to care what he was doing."

De Coursier was still running his hotel and tavern when he died suddenly in 1865, leaving his wife with three young boys. When she died 10 years after that, the brothers — Robert, Edward, and Henry — were on their own. Over the next couple of years, they often had a housekeeper, Elizabeth Grant, to clean and cook for them. They also continued to operate the hotel.

"The customers would call for Robert to attend the bar for them," Grant said. "He was well liked ... The brothers seemed to live comfortably and happily together until the soda water business."

The "soda water business" would not be the only trigger for what was to come, but it was certainly the catalyst for the ill will between Robert and Edward.

* * *

Soda water had its origins in the mineral spring water popular for centuries in Europe. Its natural effervescence came from the carbon dioxide gas it obtained as it travelled up from underground springs. Not until 1767 did someone in England manage to produce the first drinkable glass of soda water. It soon became apparent that flavoured soda water could be made by adding syrups to the spring water, and the first of these was lemon in 1838. By 1850, many more flavours had appeared and patents began to emerge for soda fountains. The most famous of all soda syrups, Coca-Cola, was invented in May 1886. Mixed with regular water, it was marketed as a "brain and nerve tonic." It didn't take long before someone discovered the syrup tasted great in soda water — and the rest is history.

* * *

At the beginning of 1877, the two oldest De Coursiers, Robert and Edward, decided to make their fortunes by buying a soda fountain. Almost immediately, small quarrels between the two began. Robert felt Edward spent too much money travelling with the soda water they made. Edward complained that Robert did not work hard enough at the business. As fast as the soda water flowed, so the bad blood began to collect. Finally Robert offered to buy Edward out and gave his brother a note promising to pay for his share within the year. In truth, it seemed to be Robert who was much more financially responsible than his brother. This was certainly how the housekeeper, Elizabeth Grant, saw it.

"I was there for $1.50 a week. Between the two brothers, the bargain was made with me," Grant said. "Ordinarily, in making his bargains, Robert was sensible. He was good in making his payments. My last wages I did not receive for a year after I left them. It was his brother Edward caused this. Robert was always punctual in settling. I say he was an honest, upright honourable young man as far as could be ... He was never quarrelsome. He was very gentle."

There was another reason, too, for the tension between Robert and Edward. By May 1877, Robert had been "keeping company" with Mary Mills for almost two years, the last one of which they became engaged. However, when he had to leave to spend that summer working in Meadowvale (now North Mississauga), Edward started wooing Mary. Initially, Edward "made promises" to her, but when Mary became pregnant she learned that he had only "seduced" her to spite

Toronto Murders

Robert. Edward had no intention of following through on his earlier commitment to marry her.

Robert found out all of this on his return home and his broken engagement became one more reason to despise his brother. In the early months of 1878, housekeeper Elizabeth Grant began to notice some changes in Robert.

"He would give great sighs sometimes and say he did not see what there was to live for," Grant said. "He complained at times of the back of his head very much. He wished me to shower his head with cold water. He used to bring the large stable sponge to me and get me to shower his head, the back of it, with cold water. I did that until I would get tired — 20 minutes probably. He would generally then go out in the air ... I remember doing that at least half-a-dozen times.

"When he had the severe pains in his head, he looked wild and irritable like ... [but] after one of these attacks in his head, he was in high spirits. He was more of a moving, racing sort of fellow — restless."

After the baby was born in April 1878, Robert did go to see Mary and tried to make some arrangement between Edward and Mary for the baby to be taken care of. Edward refused to do anything.

* * *

By the end of 1878, any semblance of civility between Robert and Edward was gone. The two of them and their youngest

My Brother's Keeper

brother, Henry, all went their separate ways. Robert moved about 10 kilometres down Dundas Street to the centre of Toronto and started working with John Parker, manufacturing soda water. Henry relocated to Newmarket about 50 kilometres away, and Edward, though staying in Lambton Mills, moved to a different house. The old De Coursier homestead remained empty.

In the late summer of 1879, Edward, irritated that Robert had not yet paid him for his share in the soda fountain business, sued his brother and won. It was while Robert happened to be away hunting for a few days that September that the Sheriff went to where Robert lived and worked and seized his property. Parker, Robert's employer, would later say, "I knew of the lawsuit between his brother and him. I was at home when they came for his property, the property that was seized by his brother. He learned of the seizure from me, on his return."

In financial terms, the value of the property seized would have been barely enough to cover the costs of the Sheriff. When he found out, Robert knew Edward had launched the suit merely for spite.

The Sheriff was to sell the goods on Saturday, September 27, 1879.

Edward's actions brought about a change in Robert in the few days leading up to September 26, 1879. "I noticed that he was very despondent and down-hearted," Mary Keenan, his landlady, said. "For the first five or six months [he lived with me] he was very cheerful ... [but from] the Monday until the day [Thursday] he went away I thought he was out of sorts, in low spirits."

Parker gave Robert leave to go up to Lambton Mills for a couple of days to deal with the issue of his goods being seized. Fond of Robert, Parker would later say of him, "As long as I have known him, I would call him one of the most honourable men I ever became acquainted with."

On Thursday, September 25, Robert had lunch with Robert Stinson who owed him some money. Stinson later stated that Robert had asked him if he knew where he would get a couple of hours of shooting.

"I told him that the Humber flats was the only place I knew of." The 24-year-old man was, Stinson added, "a very sober, industrious young man."

Henry De Coursier had also come to Lambton Mills on that Thursday. Edward was overseeing the estate of their late mother and was going to sell the items in the house and divide up the books in their father's library. Henry got together with Robert for half an hour that evening before they parted. Robert went to spend the night with his old friend Samuel Bryans.

When Robert and Bryans left the house together early the next morning, with Robert carrying his gun and shot pouch, they encountered Edward along the road. Passing by each other, the brothers did not speak.

Bryans left him and Robert continued on. He walked down to the wagon shop, which was located on the north side

My Brother's Keeper

of Dundas Street. George Piggott was apprentice to the shop's owner, Alfred Chapman, and he was alone that Friday morning when Robert arrived at 8 a.m. Edward, a wagon-maker by trade, had been working at the shop until two weeks before. Assuming Edward would show up, Robert hung around the shop, sitting either on the doorstep or on the bench inside, talking with Piggott for the next hour and a half.

"We talked about different things, about shooting and one thing and another ...," Piggott would later recall. "There were a lot of butternuts [white walnuts, a popular snack at the time] in the shop. I asked him if he wanted any and he said no, he was afraid they would dirty his hands."

Robert finally left the wagon shop at 9:30 a.m. and headed to the family house. Almost as soon as he had gone, Edward appeared. "I was fixing a sulky," Piggott said. "Edward was fixing a buggy and wanted to get a pair of bands, brass bands, to go on the hubs of the light waggon [sic] he was fixing at his own place. He said he would take them down to the blacksmith's."

Piggott saw him return from the blacksmith's and walk past the shop on his way back to his own house.

In the meantime Henry had found Robert at the family's old house. Just the day before, Henry had received from Edward a share of his mother's estate. When Henry told Robert this, he said, "Robert seemed to be anxious to come to a settlement with my brother. It was about a lawsuit they had had about the soda water business."

Robert then sent Henry to tell Edward that he (Robert) would offer to pay half the expenses of the lawsuit if Edward would pay the other half — and only then would Robert settle up with Edward for the soda fountain business.

Nineteen-year-old Henry was now trapped between his warring older brothers. He took the message to Edward, but returned with the response that Edward would not do it. Robert then told Henry to take a second message to Edward, this time asking him to come up to the house to divide up the books. Henry was reluctant to do it: "I told Robert they would very likely quarrel if Edward came up. I said that because I thought so, they being on bad terms. I knew from the actions of both."

Henry delivered the message anyway, but persuaded Edward not to go. When Robert learned again from Henry that Edward was not coming, he left the house and headed down to the wagon shop again.

Arriving there, he resumed sitting on the steps. He briefly put his gun down to help Piggott turn over a sulky he was working on and then sat down again. Alfred Rook strolled by and exchanged a few words with him at 11:30 a.m. Rook continued on to Alfred Chapman's garden where the two of them were digging potatoes. Ten minutes later they heard a gunshot and Rook told Chapman someone was shooting his pigeons.

"Mr. Chapman said 'I have no pigeons. You go up and see what it is.' Then there came a second shot," Rook would later say.

My Brother's Keeper

After looking over the sulky to see what was needed for a repair, Piggott had gone back inside the shop. The west window afforded him a 100-metre view up the street. "I went to the bench, on the west side, to get some screws out of the drawer," Piggott said. "When I was there, I heard the report of a gun and I looked out the window."

He saw Edward falling with his hands up and uttering, "Oh, don't!" And then he saw Robert fire a second shot at Edward. Piggott started to run to the door, but by the time he reached the man lying face down in the dust, Robert was already striding away down the road. Piggott ran to tell Chapman and then returned to the victim. "I saw his clothes were on fire [from the gunshot] and I tried to put the fire out with my hand," Piggott said. "Then I went into the shop and got some water and poured it on his clothes and put the fire out." A neighbour, William Ireland, helped him do this and then went out into the street and started to follow Robert. He gave up when Robert went past the toll gate and into the old house. At that point, Ireland ran for Dr. Aiken.

The gunshots had attracted other neighbours by this time. "I saw Edward lying on his face," Chapman said. "We turned him over and saw he had a hole in him. We came to the conclusion that we had better take him home." Several men helped ease Edward onto a plank and they carried him to his house. He was dead by the time they got there.

While administering to Edward, Chapman had also kept an eye on Robert striding off down the street. He therefore noticed when Robert stopped, pulled what seemed to be a tiny bottle from the pocket of his trousers, and drank down the contents. Suspecting that Robert might have poisoned himself, Chapman sent Piggott to look around where Robert had been standing. In short order, Piggott found a "little druggists bottle" just inside the fence where Robert had tossed it.

The group of neighbours quickly decided to go to the De Coursier house to "secure" Robert. They searched the main floor of the house when they got there, but didn't find him. Then someone noticed stairs leading to the floor above. "I went up two steps," George Bailey later said, "and then I heard some one breathing pretty heavy. I went up three steps more and I saw [Robert] lying on a feather bed on the floor ... He was foaming at the mouth and he was unconscious. I thought he was breathing too hard and I took hold of his shirt collar and unbuttoned it and opened his shirt so that he would be enabled to get his breath easier."

Thomas Beatty, the coroner, was summoned and some medicine was given to Robert. It slowly brought him back from the brink of death. A search of the room turned up the double-barrelled gun that had been the murder weapon and a revolver Robert had also carried with him. Also found were bottles of flavouring used in the soda fountain business and a small piece of paper containing a few grains of strychnine.

The town's constable, Thomas Ide, arrived at 4 p.m. to arrest Robert, who was still "in a kind of stupor." As soon

My Brother's Keeper

as Robert began to show signs of consciousness, Ide began questioning him. "I asked him about his brother, if he knew what he had been doing." Robert, his voice quiet and his words slurred, said yes, according to Ide. "I asked him what made him do it. He said he was provoked to do it."

Robert was taken to jail and the trial, originally scheduled for January, was held over to the spring assizes in April 1880. In the months between the murder and the trial, Robert's physical and mental state seemed to deteriorate and this became the focus of the defence, led by Dalton McCarthy.

The prosecution had little difficulty in establishing that Robert had indeed shot his brother. However, McCarthy did get a witness to state that Robert had *not* spoken before his "confession" to Ide, and had to be asked the questions twice before he "mumbled" an answer. McCarthy also attacked Ide for going to a man and pumping him while he was in a stupor "in order that you might be able to come here and give evidence against him."

By mid-way through day one of the two-day trial, the defence took over. Their first strategy was to present Robert as an industrious and peaceable man, liked by everyone he met. Then they showed a pre-disposition for mental illness in the family by having witnesses relay: 1) the odd behaviour his father had exhibited, and 2) the fact that his maternal grandmother had also exhibited signs of mental illness later in her life. This established, they then made the sole focus of the defence Robert's deteriorating mental and physical condition during the time leading up to the murder and the months he spent in prison awaiting trial.

William Waites was a constable who, for four and a half months, was in charge of Robert in jail during the night. Waites kept a "little memorandum book" in which he noted Robert's condition. He stated that Robert appeared to be fine until the middle of October 1879, and after that was dull and depressed in spirits and very absent-minded. "If I asked him a question about anything, he would sometimes answer me on a totally different subject," Waites testified. In the middle of November, the prisoner began to complain of "sick headaches."

"On one or two occasions I put my hand on his head — he would ask me to put my hand on his head," Waites said. "His head was just burning hot. He did not get over that for some time … He only looked a little wild at times. I have repeated a question as much as two or three times before I would get his attention fixed."

At that time, Robert was also suffering from insomnia every night, and by early January Waites noticed that he began experiencing a great deal of twitching in his body even when he was finally able to sleep. Waites went so far as to pinch Robert one night, "very hard," to see if he was faking the twitching. Robert did not respond and stayed sound asleep. "I noticed [the twitching] more about him when he was speaking at first," Waites said. "It was his voice really was the first thing that drew my attention to it … It was more particularly on the right side. I noticed some times when he would be walking that he would walk a little lame on the right leg."

The main defence witness was Dr. Stephen Lett, the assistant superintendent of the Toronto Lunatic Asylum. He had numerous visits with Robert and gave long and precise testimony on his physical and mental states of health. "I observed he had peculiar spasmodic twitchings of the upper part of the body, of the nature of *Corea*, commonly called *St. Vitus' Dance*, which affected his speech and under which he labored very considerably," Lett told the court. "I also noticed when he was sitting on the bed, he was lopped over to one side. And, on his walking, I noticed that the same lopping over to one side remained and he walked as if lame.

"He seemed very reluctant to walk. I pressed him to do so ... After he walked up and down the length of the room two or three times, he staggered very much ... He threw himself on the bed. He appeared perfectly exhausted. His face was flushed. The twitching very much increased and he was almost unable to speak."

Lett continued that, the next day, he had noticed "intermission" in Robert's pulse. To be sure he was right about this, he even did an experiment with another man, testing his pulse. Robert's pulse, he found, was unusual: "Every twelve or fourteen beats it stopped one beat." From these physical symptoms and Robert's family history, Lett had no trouble stating, "I am of the opinion he is mentally unsound."

The cross-examination of Dr. Lett by the Crown was

aggressive as they tried to discredit the findings. Lett tried to keep calm and explained that no individual symptom had led to his diagnosis — that they all had to be taken into account, including genetic history. When Aemilius Irving, counsel for the Crown suggested that Robert had "simulated" the missed beats of his heart, Lett reached the end of his patience.

> *Irving:* "Would it be difficult to simulate them?"
>
> *Lett:* "No man in the world, as far as I know, can produce intermission in his pulse. Nor could he get up these movements, these twitchings that have been described."
>
> *Irving:* "Don't you think he could have made these grimaces all the time you were there?"
>
> *Lett:* "Have you observed them?"
>
> *Irving:* "I have not."
>
> *Lett:* "Then, why do you say that?"

The defence also produced Dr. Charles Berryman, who had been called in to examine Robert in October 1879, a couple of weeks after the murder. Berryman's conclusion was that "some irritation of the brain existed, whether whole or partial I cannot say, but irritation of the brain undoubtedly existed. And the man is, I think, insane."

My Brother's Keeper

Although many had known of the soda fountain business and that Edward had had Robert's goods seized, there was a witness who supplied information that no-one had known about until the trial — Mary Mills. She testified in court to her engagement to Robert and her subsequent seduction and abandonment by Edward.

The jury retired for close to three hours before returning to say they could not reach a verdict. The judge urged them to continue trying. In 45 minutes they had one: guilty. Robert De Coursier was sentenced to hang June 16, 1880, only six weeks away. Thousands of petitions for commutation were launched, but none were successful. Robert was told on June 14 that there would be no reprieve. His brother Henry then petitioned the jail for Robert's body to be released to him after the hanging.

* * *

Robert was watched day and night because he had frequently promised to cheat the hangman. Only the six people closest to him, including Henry, visited him in the last week of his life. The day watchman came on at 7 a.m. on June 15, 1880, and spoke to Robert who seemed cheerful. At 8 a.m., Robert rose and went behind the screen to use the commode and then drank some water out of a pitcher afterwards. He immediately returned to bed and a minute later the guard heard a gurgling sound coming from his throat. When he realized his prisoner was close to death, he banged on the cell door and called for help. It was too late. Death had come within three minutes. Authorities discovered "a small phial in the commode in the prisoner's cell."

If Robert had been hung, the law would have required him to be buried on the prison grounds. In this case, his body was released and his remains were interred in the churchyard of St. George's Church in Lambton Mills.

The inquest found nowhere to lay the blame and the coroner's jury concluded "that Robert William De Coursier came to his death on the fifteenth day of June ... at the said gaol from the effects of a certain poison, to wit prussic or hydrocyanic acid, administered by himself with the intent to commit suicide. The jury find that the said poison was contained in a small bottle clandestinely given to the said deceased at the gaol since his sentence with intent that the said prisoner should thereby commit suicide, but how, or by what means the said bottle was so given to the prisoner, the jury are unable to say."

* * *

Was it just jealousy or brotherly conflict that drove Robert to do what he did? Did Edward really push him too far? Or was Robert doomed from the beginning to a sad end? Did the demons that claimed his father eat away at him too? No one will ever know the answer for certain, but one might speculate ...

My Brother's Keeper

Following Robert's first suicide attempt after Edward's murder, the coroner found on Robert some tin-type photographs of himself as a small boy with his father — perhaps a man he identified with too closely.

And the following testimony that the high constable of York County gave at Robert's murder trial perhaps points to a die that was already cast. In describing the results of the inquest into Robert's father's death, the constable stated: "The following is the verdict rendered by the jury: 'That the said John De Coursier came to his death by swallowing a large quantity of Prussic acid, while greatly excited and while labouring under temporary insanity.' It is dated on the 25th June, 1865."

Chapter 6
Death by Alcohol

Beware of intemperance, for it's a curse
It destroys the soul and empties the purse.
It fills the prisons, fills the heart with woe,
It defaces beauty, and will be your overthrow.

Martin Richard Kehoe, 1854

hen Martin Richard Kehoe, 42, woke up at 2 p.m. on Sunday, July 30, 1854, he was alone in his bed. He was still fully dressed, including his boots. The house was very quiet. Turning to look next to him on the bed, he was surprised that his wife, Ellen, wasn't there. His memory was very foggy and the effects of alcohol still heavy on his body. Martin lay there for a minute trying to think. It was his normal custom, "when in liquor," to get up in the middle of the night in a search for more alcohol. He was sure he had not done that.

Death by Alcohol

He dragged himself out of bed and staggered into the kitchen. He met with a horrible sight. Ellen, 37, lay on the floor with her throat cut, the blood pooling around her.

"You may well suppose how I felt; I can scarcely tell myself now how I felt," Martin was soon to write in a story of his life.

"I ran to her, raised her in my arms either once or twice, I found she was dead" he said. "Whether she was cold or not I don't know; where she had the wounds, unless what I heard, I don't know; how the razor lay, or in what position, I don't know; whether she had a cap on, or not I don't know; what dress she had on I don't know. One thing I observed she lay in a crooked position. I remember seeing blood, but don't know how much. I am positive of never seeing her move a muscle, leg or arm, nor change a word with me from taking the first glass of grog the night before."

There was a lot Martin didn't know of the events leading to her death, but the one thing he knew for sure was that Ellen was dead.

* * *

Martin Kehoe was born to Irish parents in Hull, England, on July 18, 1812. His father, a non-commissioned officer in the British Army, was stationed at Hull, but the family was eventually stationed in the town of Carlow in Ireland.

"I was a wild boy in my juvenile days," recounted Martin

Toronto Murders

in his story, "but much brighter with regard to intellect than the younger members of our family. When I was considered inclined to take a trade, I was sent to the metropolitan city, Dublin, where I was apprenticed, in the year 1830, to learn the art of a boot and shoe maker." He served a five-year apprenticeship and, upon completion, sailed for Liverpool. His time there went well and he was, by his own words, "never the slightest intoxicated from liquor."

In October 1835, Martin's father retired after 39 years in the army and asked his oldest son to come home to Carlow. Martin had a brother slightly younger than he who had just completed his apprenticeship in the same trade, and his father wanted all the family to live together in Dublin so that Martin and his brother could teach boot- and shoemaking to the two youngest brothers. Martin agreed and went ahead to Dublin to set things up. On his way there, he "had more than was necessary of that cursed and soul-destroying draught," the first sign of problems to come.

The family settled in together and, when his father died the following year, Martin took on the responsibilities for the remainder of the family. By 1840, the two youngest Kehoe boys had joined the army and Martin's only sister had married.

The next three years passed relatively happily, with Martin's mother keeping house for him and his remaining brother. "I had now seen the great comfort of being a temperate man" Martin later wrote, though adding that he

Death by Alcohol

"used once in a time to take a day or two on what is called a 'spree.'"

He met Ellen on June 10, 1843, when she spent the evening at the Kehoe home enjoying Martin's musical talents. Born Ellen Keyley to Roman Catholic parents who died when she was very young, Ellen was placed in an orphanage and her last name changed to Ross. She became, and was raised, a Protestant from that point forward. Martin's mother became very attached to Ellen and encouraged a relationship between the two. She was successful, and Martin and Ellen were married in the Church of England on August 7, 1843. Some time later, Ellen volunteered to become a Catholic. Martin said later on that he had not minded either way.

The year after their wedding, Martin opened a boot- and shoemaking shop of his own. The business did well because his work was very good. However, the first signs of trouble in their marriage began to appear.

"It was here I first found my wife was really fond of drink," he wrote. "I have not the slightest doubt had I restrained the woman from drink, and that I myself was a sober man, that she at least would not be anything like what she was ... When I did not take drink I never knew her to take it, but as soon as I commenced she commenced also."

A daughter was born to Martin and Ellen in June 1844, followed soon by a son. Martin's brother had emigrated to the United States, and so Martin's mother lived with Martin and Ellen. The family seemed to be thriving and happy, aided perhaps by the fact that Martin was being "temperate and industrious." Things would never be as good for the Kehoes again.

* * *

The Great Famine hit Ireland and crops failed. Because the working classes could not afford food, let alone new boots or shoes, Martin decided to move the family to Liverpool. They went, leaving his mother to live with his sister.

It was not long afterwards that Martin made the even bigger decision — like thousands of other Irish did at that time — to head for the United States.

"On the 21st July, 1847" he wrote, "we sailed from Liverpool in the ship Virgilla [*Virgilia*], commandeered by Captain Barr [S. Barre]." Martin, knowing the trip would be a long one, stocked many provisions for the family. Early one morning, more than a month into the journey, the ship was caught in a high wind with too much sail up. Knocked on its side with its gunwales underwater, it stayed like that for six minutes during which there was much terror and confusion among the passengers below deck. "I took my girl in my arms, the mother, the boy. Said I, without moving from my berth, if she goes down we will all go down together." Fortunately, the ship eventually righted itself and the trip resumed.

"A respectable woman in the opposite berth to me was immediately confined" wrote Martin, "and delivered of a son;

Death by Alcohol

they both died and I saw them thrown down into the deep sea the following morning. We had nine more who shared the same fate. It was indeed a melancholy sight to see."

On September 20, 1847, the Kehoes arrived "at quarantine" on Grosse Île, in the St. Lawrence River, not far from Quebec City.

"When we landed on this barren and pestilential island both my children were sick. I looked around me and as there was only sheds for the emigrants and one store, I went to the latter, purchased what I thought most essential, and made ourselves as happy as we could under such trying circumstances. There was great numbers dying; indeed every one had sorrow depicted in their countenance for the loss of their relatives.

"We were five days on this solitary island, and here was misery to be seen in the extreme; whole families carried before their just God in the space of three days."

* * *

Grosse Île was a quarantine station that, in 1847 and 1848, was filled to overflowing as a result of the famine in Ireland. The conditions on board the hundreds of ships that arrived were deplorable. Hundreds died before reaching land, and thousands died within days of arriving on the island. The main cause of death was typhus, but poor nutrition and harsh living conditions (mainly due to the sheer numbers of

Quarantine station at Grosse Île, Quebec, ca. 1890 – 1910

immigrants) made a bad situation worse. The owners of the passenger ships were also to blame, for they tended to carry many more people than they were allowed to. The government downplayed the numbers of dead, so official numbers have never been accurate. No one knows exactly how many on Grosse Île died in 1847 and 1848 (most of whom were Irish), but it was likely upwards of 20,000. In 1909, a monument was erected on the western end of Grosse Île and bore Irish, English, and French inscriptions. The one in

Death by Alcohol

Gaelic reads: "Children of the Gael died in their thousands on this island having fled from the laws of the foreign tyrants and an artificial famine in the years 1847–1848. God's loyal blessing upon them. Let this monument be a token to their name and honour from the Gaels of America. God save Ireland."

On September 25, 1847, an order went out for all the passengers who had come in on the *Virgilia* to board the ship again as they were going on to Montreal. In a way they were lucky because many of the earlier ships in the summer were quarantined for weeks (a contributing factor in the number of deaths reported among the ships' passengers). With not enough sheds for them on land, the healthy were left aboard the vessels with the sick — and, not surprisingly, many of them became sick, too, and died. Getting off the island had its sorrows too: "Here was the heart-rending scene! Parents obliged to leave their offspring behind them, and children obliged to leave their dead parents," Martin wrote.

And so it was for Martin and Ellen. Their daughter had been hospitalized with illness when they learned their ship would be leaving the island to continue the trip to Montreal. "On hearing of the sudden route," wrote Martin, "I went direct to Doctor Douglas, who was head physician on the Island, respecting my child; he gave me liberty to see her, and said if she recovered she would be taken good care of and sent to me in any part of the Province I would be in, when the Navigation would open up in the Spring. I shall never forget how I felt to leave this child; she was my first, and was my favourite; although my son resembled me much more, this little one I was much attached to, and the loss of her often caused me to drink after coming to Canada."

* * *

After they reached Montreal, Martin found work in his trade to be scarce and the pay worse. He decided to take Ellen and his baby son to Kingston, but they were only able to make it as far as Lachine (just west of Montreal) because the Lachine Canal was under repair. (Before the construction of the St. Lawrence Seaway, the Lachine Canal was the main entrance to the canal network linking the Atlantic Ocean to the centre of the continent.) It was dark and windy on their arrival and Martin could find nowhere for them to sleep.

"The sheds were all crowded, so that we were obliged to make our bed and lie down in an open one exposed to the chilly blast of the night air," he wrote. "On the following morning my wife found her baby dead by her side." After finding someone to build a small coffin, they buried their son in the afternoon and then sailed for Kingston.

Ellen was very sick by the time they landed there and, fearing typhus, Martin could not find them accommodation. As often happened to recent shipboard arrivals, the Board of Health finally ordered Ellen to hospital.

"After she went I became almost delirious, in a strange country, far from those who would give me kind

Death by Alcohol

consolation," Martin said. He began to drink, even taking some spirits to the hospital for his wife. He worked for a few days, but then became sick himself and ended up in the same hospital as Ellen for 10 days. Both finally recovered and their luck seemed to turn for a while to the better. Martin found good work at his trade and was able to afford a furnished room for him and Ellen. "I lived in Kingston eight months, and could do well there," he wrote — but added soberly, "if we only let the grog be still."

As soon as the canal opened in the spring, Martin tried to find out what happened to his daughter. He received no definitive answer, although the authorities told him it was likely the little girl had died at Grosse Île.

"Men oftentimes, and women too, take drink to kill grief, but I really believe it adds more to it than it diminishes it," he said. Ellen was drinking heavily and had an affair, but when Martin "proposed to her a divorcement," she would not hear of it. They sailed for Montreal on June 1, 1848, with the purpose of finding their daughter. He spent two days after his arrival looking over the lists of the dead children and the names of those that went into welfare. His daughter's name did not show up on any of the lists. At that point, he and Ellen "gave up all hopes" and moved to St. John's, Newfoundland. They lived above a tavern, and one day Martin came home to find his wife there, drunk in bed, and two soldiers in the room. Their relationship survived this incident but Martin and Ellen were on a downhill run.

Toronto Murders

* * *

In June 1849, they sailed for Boston, hoping to reunite with Martin's brother. It was not to be. They learned that the brother had returned to Dublin and died six months later.

Again, however, things briefly improved. Martin found good work and both he and Ellen worked hard, did not drink, and began saving money. Their reason was Ellen's pregnancy. Then in October, nearing her time of delivery, Ellen fell while hanging the laundry. Martin called the doctor the next day.

"He remained all day with her," Martin said, "and at 10 o'clock at night delivered her of two fine babies, boy and girl. Up to this I had good hopes that by having my children it would settle us down in some place."

But bad luck followed when, later that day, both babies died.

Martin managed to stay sober in the next weeks while his wife recovered, but then went on a spree and a doctor and clergyman had to be called. "From this spree I got into delirium tremens of the very worst description," he said. Ellen was soon drinking heavily again as well and having affairs.

Martin's drinking was now making him paranoid and he believed his wife and other people were trying to kill him. Ellen would often walk with him in the evenings, hoping to help the delusions go away. One night she was trying to get him to cross a bridge and head home. Martin, convinced there

Death by Alcohol

were men about who were trying to kill him, started raising a ruckus. Two watchmen nearby wanted to take him to the police station. Martin put up a fight and was, as he later put it, "struck a severe blow over the right temple, cutting my cap and skull through." He was taken to the station and released in the morning, but his mind was never the same afterwards. The drinking and the delusions continued.

One day, Ellen brought home a woman whom Martin considered to be an "improper person." In a rage, he stabbed Ellen — not fatally, it turned out, but he was sent to prison for 18 months in spite of her plea to the judge that he was insane and out of his mind. This would have ended most marriages, but the Kehoes' proved stronger than that.

"We corresponded, she came to see me, and when I came out we lived together," Martin wrote. "I met this woman with as much feeling of good nature when I saw her as if there was never anything between us. She received me the same."

* * *

Although Ellen still drank heavily after his release, Martin — for the moment — stopped. They decided to return to Canada, arriving there on September 9, 1852. Almost immediately, for whatever reason, both hit the bottle. They continued to work well together at his trade (Ellen being a boot-binder) and had no quarrels, but Ellen's drinking was becoming more of a problem. Partly for this reason, Martin felt compelled to try the United States once more — a venture that was almost over before it began. On the day they arrived in March 1854, Martin sent Ellen off to buy some food. When she did not return, he went looking for her. He found her drunk in a hayloft of the stable attached to the hotel where they were staying. He took her back to their room and the next day they returned (for what would be the final time) to Toronto.

Martin wrote that from then until the beginning of July 1854, "I drank no grog; neither did my wife to my knowledge." At that point, having saved money, they were able to buy some furniture and moved into a house on Sumach Street on July 11. Seemingly unable to handle prosperity, however, their resolve to stay off the bottle fell apart once more and they began to drink very heavily. In fact, Martin only worked one out of the next three weeks because of his bingeing. His memories of what was to be the last week of Ellen's life were completely blurred and he was plagued with delirium tremens. "The greatest part of this week I cannot in any way, bring to mind how we spent it," he wrote. "I never remember being so stupid with regard to my memory when I had delirium tremens before."

In the past, he could always remember later what took place while he was on a bender, but this time he was at a loss to remember anything of that week. He did recall that on July 30, in the evening, the two of them went to a tavern and Ellen "got some drink in a jar and carried it home with her."

Death by Alcohol

Martin's paranoia had returned and he thought they were being watched or followed. He poured himself a drink and this is the last thing he remembered before waking up in bed the next afternoon.

On finding Ellen's body, he ran to his landlord's apartment, which was immediately beside theirs. Thomas Mitchell owned the house on Sumach Street, near Queen.

"I told him to come in with me, that my wife was after cutting her throat," Martin said.

Mitchell, recounting this in court, said of Martin, "His hands were all blood, and his shirt. My wife asked how that happened, and he said his wife had cut her throat and that he had lifted her up. I went to the door and looked in and saw enough. I then ran for the police and by the time I had returned there were a number of persons there."

The panicked husband had also run to another neighbour for help, so many people had collected in the house by the time the authorities showed up. It did not take much to realize that suicide could not have taken place. The floors of both rooms had blood on them. A razor covered with blood and hair was found a few feet away from the body. It was broken in half. There was a trail of blood from the floor in the bedroom to the place where Ellen lay. Blood had also flowed heavily from the body. One heavy cut severed the windpipe halfway through and cut into the base of the neck. On the left side, the gash went from the back of the neck and around to the windpipe, ending a few centimetres lower than the other one. The coroner, Dr. King, was called in and he declared firmly it was not suicide.

Martin was quickly arrested and an inquest called that evening. It was short, and the coroner's jury returned a verdict of wilful murder against him. Believing that Martin's defence team at a future trial would claim that the alcohol caused him to kill Ellen, Dr. King stated he did not think Martin had been "under the influence" when the murder took place. While Martin could not remember what happened that night, one thing he knew for sure was that he'd been beyond intoxicated.

"After all had been over," wrote Martin recalling the inquest, "Dr. King states I said I thanked him and the [coroner's] jury for returning a just verdict. If the learned Doctor had not considered me labouring under delirium tremens, why did he order me brandy twice? If this statement had been made, it appears to me that it was highly wrong to take cognizance of what any man said labouring under my great affliction of mind. Such words I had no intention of stating, nor could I have done with justice to myself."

Martin's trial took place on October 20, 1854. On hearing there was some ill feeling against him because Ellen had converted to Catholicism for him, R. Dempsey, Martin's lawyer, recommended that the accused man challenge the jury selection. Martin chose not to, saying, "As I left her to her own free will, I left them also to theirs, without a challenge. Love your neighbour, no matter what his religion may be,

Death by Alcohol

and direct your children to do so; for the man who is bigoted in his heart against his fellow man for differing in opinion of religion, is a bad man, and the truth is not in him."

Two doctors testified about the wounds and their belief they could not have been self-inflicted. However, because the couple lived in such close proximity to their landlord, Martin always felt they would have heard something if he and Ellen had struggled. The doctors provided one of the answers. "The power of crying for assistance was prevented by the infliction of either of the wounds," coroner Dr. King said. He also explained why suicide was not possible. "It is perfectly impossible from the character of the wounds that the person could have lived after either of them so that it is impossible the person could have inflicted them both herself."

Thomas Mitchell did testify that he and his wife never heard any angry words or fighting between the Kehoes and heard absolutely no sound that Saturday night or the Sunday morning.

Dempsey also pointed out that Martin had no motive and nothing to gain by this murder. He also stressed that when Martin found his wife dead, he did not run away which he would have most likely done had he been guilty of the murder. But Dempsey's was a losing battle. The jury was only out a short time before returning with a guilty verdict.

"I received the verdict with as much good will of heart to my fellow man as I did my sentence," Martin said. A sentence of death would be carried out December 5, 1854.

Toronto Murders

Martin wrote it would be easier to accept if he could only remember what had happened, "but on this melancholy occasion all my endeavours have been in vain in trying to bring to mind the cause of my wife's death." One of his regrets was that he did not divorce Ellen. "There seems to me to be a chain to which we were both linked, not to be easily separated ... Hence this strong chain of affection, or something else over which I seemed to have no control, linked us on step by step, until the unhappy event occurred."

In the weeks leading up to his execution, Martin had the daily support of Reverend T. Fitzhenry. He also decided to write the story of his life to be published after his death. His goal was both to help his own soul and that of others afflicted by an addiction to alcohol. Those reading it, he said, "must admit that intemperance has been the leading artery to all my unhappiness and misfortunes."

Martin also wrote a short version of his history and read it to the 2000 people who had gathered in the inclement December weather to watch him hang. "I feel happy in my mind," he closed. "I have spoken the truth from first to last as far as I was able to bring my conscience and mind touching her death."

Handing his entire manuscript to Reverend Fitzhenry, Martin Kehoe mounted the gallows and, *The Globe and Mail* reported, "met his doom with all that stoicism which has marked his conduct since he was first apprehended on the charge of murdering his wife."

Death by Alcohol

*Of all deeds I've done I must repent;
For the one I have to die I am innocent.
As far as I remember I do not know
Of taking the life of Ellen Kehoe.*

Martin Richard Kehoe, 1854

Further Reading

Atwood, Margaret. *Alias Grace*. Toronto, ON: McClelland & Stewart, 1996.

Strange, Carolyn. *Toronto's Girl Problem: The Perils and Pleasures of the City, 1880–1930*. Toronto, ON: University of Toronto Press, 1995.

Strange, Carolyn. *True Crime, True North: The Golden Age of Canadian Pulp Magazines*. Vancouver, BC: Raincoast Books, 2004.

Toronto Telegram. Landmarks of Toronto. Volumes I & II. Toronto, ON: J. Ross Robertson, 1894/1896.

Photo Credits

Cover: CP Images; National Archives of Canada: pages 53 (PA-130009), 68 (PA-166917), 76 (C-002107460), 114 (PA-046790).

Acknowledgements

I am always thankful to the writers who came before me, leaving me a trail of history to follow in news clippings, magazine articles, and books. I hope my own words linger as long.

I want to sincerely thank the people at the National Archives of Canada in Ottawa. Their help allowed me to find the trial transcripts and other research material I needed.

Thanks as well to the librarians at the Vancouver Public Library, Central Branch, who enabled me to find a few missing pieces of information. The materials from the past that I was able to find in the Toronto Reference library were also invaluable.

A special note of thanks to all the court reporters of the past, whose diligence has allowed me to read exactly the words said during trials that took place more than a hundred years ago.

To Altitude Publishing — thanks for your continued support and encouragement.

To my editor, Georgina Montgomery — you are the best catcher that a pitcher could ever ask for and I cannot imagine going through this process with anyone else.

Many thanks to all the cats in my life who have supported both me and my writing — you know who you are.

About the Author

Susan McNicoll lives in Vancouver, British Columbia. Although she is now a die-hard British Columbian, her heart still belongs to the Toronto Blue Jays. Susan lived in downtown Toronto for 17 years and it is to that city that she returns for her fourth book in the Amazing Stories series. Susan's lifelong love of words and history has been the main focus of her writing career, which began with the five years she spent as a reporter for the *Ottawa Journal* in the 1970s. Her book about the history of postwar Canadian theatre, *Everyman Had Its Day*, is due to be published in 2005 by Ronsdale Press. Although her published work to date has been in the nonfiction realm, Susan is currently working on a series of fairy tales based on the four seasons of healing.

Amazing Author Question and Answer

What was your inspiration for writing about Toronto murders?

With all the murder books I've written, my inspiration was the same: I found people whose stories I wanted to tell and who had something, I thought, to teach us all.

What surprised you most while you were researching Toronto murders?

As always, it is a tremendous shock to me that times change but individuals, for the most part, do not. The same emotions drive our actions now as they did then.

What do you most admire about the person or people in this Amazing Story?

How resilient the people who lived in those times were. We are most privileged to live in Canada in the twenty-first century. Life was hard 100–150 years ago, especially for women.

What escapade do you most identify with?

I love the story of Frederick Capreol and his efforts to go after, and capture, the killers of his friend Thomas Kinnear.

Toronto Murders

What difficulties did you run into when researching this topic?

I like to ensure my stories are as accurate as possible, so it is always a challenge to track down information from as close to the source as possible.

What part of the writing process did you enjoy most?

Every part of it. I always think I love the research the most while I am doing it because I get so excited. Then I start to weave the story together and I think I like that part the best because it is a challenge to put all the information together. By the time I have finished writing a book, I am exhausted and I think I like that part the best — actually finishing the project!

Why did you become a writer? Who inspired you?

When I finished school, I had no idea what I was going to do with my life. I spent a year after university working in a department store and saving money to travel for four months in Europe in 1972. One night in a youth hostel there, I sat up with a jolt. At that moment, for reasons I have never understood, I was convinced beyond a shadow of a doubt that I was going to become a writer.

Amazing Author Question and Answer

What is your next project?

One, revising and adding to *Everyman Had Its Day*, a history/biography of early post-World War II professional theatre in Canada. It is scheduled to be published late in 2005. And two, writing a book that grew out of one of the murders I wrote about in *British Columbia Murders* (Altitude, 2003).

Who are your Canadian heroes?

As far as writers go, Margaret Laurence. Others include Terry Fox, who fulfilled in his short life the purpose for which he was born; and all the early post-World War II actors who struggled, with virtually no compensation, to bring professional theatre to stages across Canada.

Which other Amazing Stories would you recommend?

Amazing Stories are truly a smorgasbord of history and personalities. Just glance through the titles and you are bound to find something to pique your interest. However, if you like true crime and history, read my other titles in the series — *British Columbia Murders* (2003), *Ontario Murders* (2004), and *Jack the Ripper* (2005).

AMAZING STORIES
by the same author!

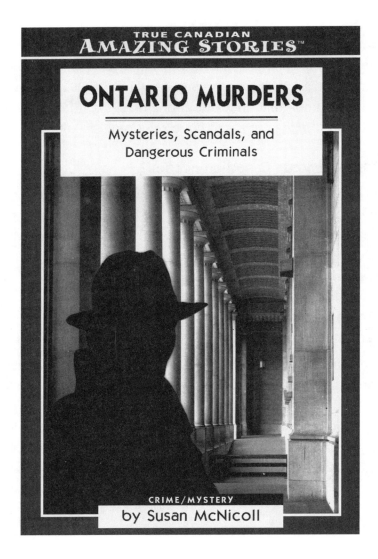

ONTARIO MURDERS
Mysteries, Scandals, and Dangerous Criminals

"From an early age, lying came easily to her. Everything she did was a performance, a role she played to create an illusion."

Six chilling stories of notorious Ontario murders are recounted in this spine-tingling collection. From the pretty but dangerous Evelyn Dick to the mysterious murder of one of the Fathers of Confederation, Thomas D'Darcy McGee, these stories will keep you on the edge of your seat.

 True stories. Truly Canadian.

ISBN 1-55153-951-9

AMAZING STORIES

by the same author!

BRITISH COLUMBIA MURDERS
Mysteries, Crimes, and Scandals

"More than 30 wounds had been dug into her body with a knife... For more than 50 years, the police would be virtually certain who her murderer was, but would never charge him. Why?

Lock your doors and draw your curtains... Six of British Columbia's most notorious murders are recounted in these gripping stories of betrayal and intrigue. From the tragic murder of Molly Justice to the unsolved mystery of Janet Smith's untimely death, these stories will keep you on the edge of your seat.

 True stories. Truly Canadian.

ISBN 1-55153-963-2

AMAZING STORIES
by the same author!

AMAZING STORIES™

JACK THE RIPPER

Murder, Mystery and Intrigue
in London's East End

HISTORY/CRIME
by Susan McNicoll

JACK THE RIPPER
Murder, Mystery and Intrigue in London's East End

"London lies today under the spell of a great terror. A nameless reprobate – half beast, half man – is at large, who is daily gratifying his murderous instincts on the most miserable and defenceless classes."
The Star, September 1888

In the 1880s, the East End of London became the staging place for a series of bloodcurdling murders that caused outrage and widespread panic throughout the nation. Although many criminologists have speculated as to the identity of the killer, to this day the murderer is known only as Jack the Ripper. The tale of his four-month reign of terror is told in this gripping story.

 True stories. Truly Canadian.

ISBN 1-55265-900-3

AMAZING STORIES
ALSO AVAILABLE!

TRUE CANADIAN AMAZING STORIES™

PRAIRIE MURDERS

Mysteries, Crimes, and Scandals

CRIME/MYSTERY

by Peter Smith

PRAIRIE MURDERS
Mysteries, Crimes, and Scandals

"The devil told me to kill Martin Sitar and all his family, and then go away and hide in the bushes."
Mass-murderer Thomas Hreshkoski

Seven chilling stories of murders across the Prairies are recounted in this gripping collection. Not for the faint-hearted, these stories tell of violence and bloodshed, as well as the police investigations that led to the eventual capture of the perpetrators. From the "Ductman of Drumheller" to the murder of Banff cabbie Lucie Turmel, these true stories will keep you on the edge of your seat.

 True stories. Truly Canadian.

ISBN 1-55439-050-8

AMAZING STORIES
ALSO AVAILABLE!

TRUE CANADIAN AMAZING STORIES®

DEADLY WOMEN OF ONTARIO

Murderous Tales of Deceit and Treachery

HISTORY/CRIME
by Cheryl MacDonald

DEADLY WOMEN OF ONTARIO
Murderous Tales of Deceit and Treachery

"It wasn't until Mary was led to the scaffold and the rope was placed about her neck that she cried out, as though finally realizing that she was going to hang."

Women in Canada frequently got away with murder and escaped the hangman's noose. A few were not so fortunate. The first woman hanged in Upper Canada was Mary Osborn, who was executed for murdering her husband. Her gruesome story and those of seven other deadly women are told in this collection of spine-chilling tales from Ontario.

 True stories. Truly Canadian.

ISBN 1-55439-026-5

AMAZING STORIES
ALSO AVAILABLE!

AMAZING STORIES™

THE MAD TRAPPER

The Incredible Tale of a Famous Canadian Manhunt

HISTORY/CRIME

by Hélèna Katz

THE MAD TRAPPER
The Incredible Tale of a Famous Canadian Manhunt

"His lips were curled back in an ugly sneer, and his teeth looked like fangs sticking out through his beard. Johnson hadn't found the peace in death that had eluded him in the last weeks of his life.

This is the incredible story of Canada's largest manhunt. Hundreds of men spent 7 weeks tracking the elusive Albert Johnson for 240 kilometres across the frozen North. He was eventually caught and killed but the identity of Albert Johnson, the Mad Trapper of Rat River, remains a mystery to this day.

 True stories. Truly Canadian.

ISBN 1-55439-026-5

OTHER AMAZING STORIES

ISBN	Title	ISBN	Title
1-55153-959-4	A War Bride's Story	1-55153-951-9	Ontario Murders
1-55153-794-X	Calgary Flames	1-55153-790-7	Ottawa Senators
1-55153-947-0	Canada's Rumrunners	1-55153-960-8	Ottawa Titans
1-55153-966-7	Canadian Spies	1-55153-945-4	Pierre Elliot Trudeau
1-55153-795-8	D-Day	1-55153-981-0	Rattenbury
1-55153-972-1	David Thompson	1-55153-991-8	Rebel Women
1-55153-982-9	Dinosaur Hunters	1-55153-995-0	Rescue Dogs
1-55153-970-5	Early Voyageurs	1-55153-985-3	Riding on the Wild Side
1-55153-798-2	Edmonton Oilers	1-55153-974-8	Risk Takers and Innovators
1-55153-968-3	Edwin Alonzo Boyd	1-55153-956-X	Robert Service
1-55153-996-9	Emily Carr	1-55153-799-0	Roberta Bondar
1-55153-961-6	Étienne Brûlé	1-55153-997-7	Sam Steele
1-55153-791-5	Extraordinary Accounts of Native Life on the West Coast	1-55153-954-3	Snowmobile Adventures
		1-55153-971-3	Stolen Horses
		1-55153-952-7	Strange Events
1-55153-993-4	Ghost Town Stories	1-55153-783-4	Strange Events and More
1-55153-992-6	Ghost Town Stories II	1-55153-986-1	Tales from the West Coast
1-55153-984-5	Ghost Town Stories III	1-55153-978-0	The Avro Arrow Story
1-55153-973-X	Great Canadian Love Stories	1-55153-943-8	The Black Donnellys
		1-55153-942-X	The Halifax Explosion
1-55153-777-X	Great Cat Stories	1-55153-994-2	The Heart of a Horse
1-55153-946-2	Great Dog Stories	1-55153-944-6	The Life of a Loyalist
1-55153-773-7	Great Military Leaders	1-55153-787-7	The Mad Trapper
1-55153-785-0	Grey Owl	1-55153-789-3	The Mounties
1-55153-958-6	Hudson's Bay Company Adventures	1-55153-948-9	The War of 1812 Against the States
1-55153-969-1	Klondike Joe Boyle	1-55153-788-5	Toronto Maple Leafs
1-55153-980-2	Legendary Show Jumpers	1-55153-976-4	Trailblazing Sports Heroes
1-55153-775-3	Lucy Maud Montgomery		
1-55153-967-5	Marie Anne Lagimodière	1-55153-977-2	Unsung Heroes of the Royal Canadian Air Force
1-55153-964-0	Marilyn Bell		
1-55153-999-3	Mary Schäffer	1-55153-792-3	Vancouver Canucks
1-55153-953-5	Moe Norman	1-55153-989-6	Vancouver's Old-Time Scoundrels
1-55153-965-9	Native Chiefs and Famous Métis		
		1-55153-990-X	West Coast Adventures
1-55153-962-4	Niagara Daredevils	1-55153-987-X	Wilderness Tales
1-55153-793-1	Norman Bethune	1-55153-873-3	Women Explorers

These titles are available wherever you buy books. If you have trouble finding the book you want, call the Altitude order desk at **1-800-957-5888**, e-mail your request to: **orderdesk@altitudepublishing.com** or visit our Web site **at www.amazingstories.ca**

New **AMAZING STORIES** titles are published every month.